I'M MAGNET

I'M MAGNET

ELENA GUSHCHINA

Elena Gushchina
I'M MAGNET (Eng.)
YA – MAGNIT (Rus.) - Я – МАГНИТ (УДК 159.9 / ББК 88.3 / Г 981)

Gushchina E.
I'M MAGNET / Elena Gushchina; [Rus. YA - MAGNIT, Elena Gushchina]. – 2015. - 240 pages – Published in EU.

© Elena Gushchina, 2012
© First English edition, design. Elena Gushchina, 2015

ISBN 978-952-68354-0-2 (Paperback)
ISBN 978-952-68354-1-9 (EPUB)

immag.net
#immagnet

Learning is finding out what you already know,

Doing is demonstrating that you know it,

Teaching is reminding others that they know it as well as you do.

We are all learners, doers, and teachers.

- Richard Bach

To All of You.

With Love.

Contents

Several words

When you become acquainted with the principles of the power of thought and begin to apply this knowledge in practice, unconsciously you want to achieve the greater goals immediately and without any obstacles. Many are facing certain difficulties. Some become frustrated without seeing immediate results, and others begin to doubt the use of the power of thought itself and just like me at first, ask: "Am I not deceiving myself?"

Inspired by newer and newer discoveries, we suddenly come across the incomprehension of people around us. Why is this happening? Why do our close people sprinkle us with doubts, express their "no", do not listen to us and continue to live, to think, absolutely not following the principles and the laws of the universe?

We may think that all stages have passed, we have achieved harmony with ourselves, but we again find ourselves in the situations, which rouse us to indignation. Why is this happening? With all positive thinking and a healthy lifestyle, some other obstacles are constantly appearing on our way. Does the law of attraction work in the required manner, anytime, anywhere, under any circumstances? Is it possible to affect the course of events, the development of situation quickly? Is it necessary "to take actions" and, what actions in particular must be carried out? How to find yourself and to realize your potentials? How to change your life, to find your inner power and make the images of your dreams real?

After reading the books about receiving wealth and prosperity many stuck on the path, do not dare to apply the knowledge obtained. Yes, indeed, through the power of thought it is possible to get innumerable riches, achieve the highest results, realize the most daring desires, but there are some conditions, on which this all can come true. Together we will walk the path, go up to the required level of the consciousness, which will contribute to the understanding of your inner strength, gaining confidence and balance, so essential for the successful materialization of the desired.

Let me share my experience with you. More than a decade I consciously use the power of thought, and I would like to give you a deeper understanding of the existing laws on my own example, to inspire you to desire and to fulfil your dreams through the wider consciousness.

" I'm Magnet" will answer the thrilling questions, will help to look at ourselves from different point of view. You will recognize some familiar situations and will see how they are influenced by the power of thought and love, which can change the subsequent course of events. You will understand everything that had happened to you, up to the reasons for the random encounters with some particular people. You will find a way to live in a harmony with the world around you and begin to consciously apply different methods and techniques, based on the author's experience.

"I'm Magnet" will reveal how to work with thoughts through clear and easy examples from everyday and ordinary life. You will want to try it yourself, to see, to feel the effect of thought and consciously begin to use its power, more and more encouraged by your own experience. You will discover entire easiness and naturalness of the universal law of attraction. You will learn to apply your abilities without struggle, to set large life goals and intermediate ones, leading to them. They in particular are so necessary for the successful cooperation with the universe. And finally you will reach the summit of the law of attraction.

Insights will occur every day, even after reading this book and, therefore, I am sure you will find this small magic key that allows you to open all doors, so that your desires could materialize in the best way for you.

Having learned to control your power and energy, you will notice explicit change in yourselves: you will become more confident, stronger in spirit and will enhance your self-esteem. You will be able to influence the course of events, change your world perception and your life.

I suggest you to tune into a positive wave, turn on some pleasant music, get comfortable and prepare to start the great journey to the world of your thoughts. With a proper intention you will be able to feel the beneficial changes even during the reading of this book:

- being happy, I attract love and prosperity to myself, easily and without any doubts

Take the sources of good, light, love, happiness and health through the senses, which you will receive here, and let each positive emotion move you closer to your goals, fill you with strength and confidence.

I love you and sincerely wish you to gain some creative confidence, enthusiasm, great achievements and to increase your well-being.

Your Elena.

Magnetic power of the book

You know that the magnet possesses property to attract opposite poles or to repel bodies with the similar poles. When we say "I'm Magnet", we mean these property and power that are present in the magnetism: the attractive force. The magnetic energy in the law of attraction extends to the universe and draws to us those things, those people and those circumstances, which are similar to the vibrations of our thoughts. Everything comes into our life through the certain magnetic channel, and each person possesses the abilities to control his own life and to deliberately attract essential positive changes.

The possibilities of human brain are unlimited; it is a powerful generator that produces and sends electromagnetic waves into the external world. Thoughts are electromagnetic impulses, which create their vibrations. Energy of thought is converted into the wave, which, in its turn, is converted into a certain form of energy or material. The thought leads to the actual creation of matter, builds up a reality, interacting, thereby, with the physical world. The more attention and energy we pay to one thought or another, the more likely they will obtain their physical forms. It is through the vibrations of our thoughts, that we create our world, all events in it and our environment. A person, who is striving for fame, wealth, success and recognition, achieves his goals. When a person wishes to get something or to meet right people on his way, to create necessary circumstances – he will be provided with all this.

With a right inner attitude we can give the objects around us a magnetic quality, the quality of attraction, similar to the vibrations of the attention, paid to this object. The water will gain the healing features, jewellery box will fulfil the wishes inserted in it, and your favourite suit will always bring you luck at the presentations. For example, a stone, which reminds us about some pleasant moments spent at the sea coast, or a bracelet, so dear to our heart, will become by means of these happy emotions a talisman, an object of strength, able to fulfil the wishes.

I invite you to start practising attraction of the desired right now with a help of the object, which you are holding in your hands and which is charged by the absolute and endless power of love. Let this book, filled with beneficial magnetism, become a family or personal guide in your future internal changes and manifestation of the desires in your reality. The energy of light and creation is attached to this book, and it is deliberately filled with the force, that can encourage the materialization of your intentions. It breathes with confidence and gratitude. There are music of soul, sincere love and joy of life in this book. Due to its vibrations it is similar to the emotional balance, the spirit of creation and happiness.

The book" I'm Magnet" will become your personal object of power. You can put inside it a picture or photo of a house on the coast, for example, and this image of your dream will be loaded with the powerful force of love. Knowing that your desire is in harmony with the universal source, you will feel the protection of future achievements and faith that everything planned will happen. Adding your love, your positive emotions to this book, you will begin to trust it and will be able to achieve some incredible effects of its magnetism, up to the helping healing.

I thank you, since this is you, who have made the book "I'm Magnet" real. You have attracted it by your desire to find answers and to gain confidence that you are on the right way. I sincerely thank you for this! Interact with the book, make it alive: turn the pages over and view your writings and attached desires, filled with the miraculous powers of love and gratitude. And the title of the book, which speaks for itself, will like a magnet attract to you a rich, abundant, interesting life, full of confidence, trust and happiness. Your wishes are destined to come true. In fact, everything that has been written or is said by anyone earlier has its manifestation in our reality. Keep this in mind and use it for your wealth, health and promotion.

Statement "I'm Magnet"

'm Magnet – is the phrase that you should remember wherever you are: at the interview, on a plane, at the meeting, at the doctor, at school, even when you play with the child or communicate with your spouse. The thoughts, which appear in your head, attract exactly what you think. Keeping in mind that you are a Magnet, you will be able to control your emotions more easily, to formulate your positive expectations and desires, throwing away all fears and doubts. The greater you focus your attention on your personal magnetism, the more powerful will become the effect of statement "I'm Magnet". You will use it more confidently, and your inner need will more strongly direct your thoughts and emotions to something that you really want in your life.

The statement "I'm Magnet" is filled with the quality of magnetism. If you use it deliberately and in a positive way, you will create a favourable magnetic field, where your dreams will begin to acquire their physical forms.

The statement "I'm Magnet" will allow you to reach the level, where the vibrations will correspond to vibrations or magnetism of your desires. And when you are in the energetic harmony with the desired circumstances or the object, you will feel confidence in its materialization and will be inspired. In response, the universe will direct you and all your actions to the realization of the dream, do everything possible for its fulfilment.

How everything has begun

was born in 1976, in Kazakhstan, but before I went to school, my family had moved to Kostomuksha, the town in the north of Russia, very close to Finland. The town was built by Finns, and it wasn't allowed to enter it without special permission. It was still Soviet reality at that time, when it was forbidden to communicate with foreigners; therefore no one even thought about any Finnish goods, we simply had no idea about life abroad. I was brought in love, but, at the same time, I was very shy and had very few friends. Then came the 90s… It was not easy for me, when I became a teenager, to get to the right path. We lived from one payday to another, which sometimes we had to wait for months.

There were joy, rises, but were also failures, falls, lack of money and disappointments. In 1995 I entered Petrozavodsk Pedagogical

University, but the things turned out in a way, that I had to go to Finland for a year to study Finnish, but have stayed there for much longer.

I started my career in a foreign country from a summer job, you will not believe it, in a cemetery. We were a few students, who took care of the flowers and cleared away the fallen dry leaves. We had to carry heavy carts with the land, so by the end of the day I did not feel my feet. But nevertheless, I recall those days with warm feelings. Cemeteries in Finland are beautiful and well maintained. It is quiet and secluded there. I like the tradition, when on Christmas Eve all families go to the cemeteries and lit candles, lighting up, thereby, the memory of those who are no longer with us.

I could become an English teacher In Russia, so moving to Finland did not attract me at that time. Cultural shock, diffused perception of the life abroad did not let me even think about the opportunities offered by this wonderful country. I am grateful to my parents, who allowed me to comprehend and to decide what was more important to me. And soon, having completely accepted my new life, I started the new exciting way, growing up in the country of Santa Claus.

I had no luck in love. Now I know that it was because of my shy nature. I was not giving myself the opportunity to find true love. We get used to so many negative manifestations in our life that we simply begin to adapt to them and do not see the main thing: all this can be changed. Probably all our mistakes, experiences and personal growth are given to us so that we on our own would gradually, but confidently assemble our unique life as a puzzle. Thus, "walking on burning coals", I have gained strength, self-confidence, feeling of significance and I've met my love. It was my birthday present. I arrived to Russia for a new foreign passport, and my future husband stopped me in the corridor of the governmental institution and signed my application.

Relationship with my second half has wrapped me of pure love and let huge amount of energy release. I got a freedom to be what I am. My power to love has multiplied in a harmonious relationship and I allowed myself to be loved.

The sincerity of a soul can discover the deepest levels of consciousness, which greatly helps to increase the inner power of a person. Sincere love makes us purer and brighter, enriches and energizes us and our surroundings. We absorb the love of parents, the people around us from the birth. At any time we can take advantage of this miraculous power and mentally fill by it the space in which we find ourselves.

I am proud of my Slavic origin, of the depth of the feelings, which are cultivated in the Slavic environment, so necessary in the process of creation of the world, where love and prosperity prevail.

I'm one of those people who need to get everything and immediately. Sometimes this, of course, helped me, but sometimes it only put obstacles on my way. Such steps, as "to forgive", "to take responsibility for everything happening in your life", "to take actions", seemed unnecessary to me, and I actually did not understand their significance then. It all looked like as a waste of time to me, I needed to get the desired instantly. When I began to feel negative thoughts physically, and a massive desire literally arose like lump in my throat, as if internally something was being blocked, I understood that there still was a lot of work to be done on me and my thoughts.

Having analysed many books on psychology, on the power of thought and even Reiki spiritual practices, I suddenly understood the entire simplicity of the materialization of that desired. Not everything I read was significant, I tried to grasp only necessary phrases, but such books are also useful: one word can change the whole life.

When I started a family and an everyday life began, one of the closest and dearest people said to me: "It's your fault, that you do not have money". I have intuitively accepted this phrase in a correct way. These exact words shook me up; they helped me to realize all reasons that led to the current situation. And they switched my attention to something I really wanted. At that moment I understood, what it really meant to take responsibility for everything happening in life. Before that I had been concentrating my attention on a vicious circle: my debts and "- 1000€" per month.

"If I can affect the relationship with a thought, then why not improve the financial situation?", - I thought.

Since then, I started imagining "+1000€" with a feeling of gratitude. Paying the bills, shopping in a store, I tried to arouse a joy in myself, and later it became a habit. I began to control all expenses more wisely, refused from "extra" insurances and in principle stopped buying anything on credit. Debtor's prison is a channel, and while we draw from it, the energy of money cannot flow freely.

I cannot explain what had happened, but sufficiently soon, in two or three months, I already could feel a significant change of situation. Suddenly there was more than enough money: there emerged an opportunity to make large purchases for home and to pay out the remaining debts. In spite of increased expenses, the desired thousand Euros "continued" to appear on my bank account it the end of a month. Soon I was able even to save some money. Suddenly I realized that I could successfully visualize one more thousand …and more.

Opening a bank account page, I started noticing more and more often the exact amount of money, which I had ordered from the universe. Knowing my approximate balance, I deliberately increased it in my mind before visiting the account page, and… that exact amount of money appeared before my eyes. I should warn you: trying to trace the origin of this "gift" is useless. Money is just energy, and it appears because of our attention. On the forums you will find a lot of similar cases, and it is becoming more and more of us.

There appeared more of successful people in my circle, and it became natural to discuss different sources of income and acquisition of financial independence. By my renewed attitude to life I was able to attract more enterprising and creative individuals.

We get what we allow ourselves to have. On the bank accounts we have exactly that amount of money, which we internally can afford. If you have asked for a million, but it comes like" lump in the throat", it means, that you are blocking any possibility of having it by your prejudices about money, wealth and prosperity. Having liberated yourself from the notions "money cannot buy happiness", "money is bad", well-deserved million can materialize on your bank account.

Our energy field breaks, reacting to our negative thoughts and emotions, which leads to poor health, unhappy relationships and even to some losses. We always receive a greater extent of what we are grateful for, even if it seems insignificant to us. And we lose everything that we do not appreciate. Concentrating on insults, experiencing desperation or self-pity, criticizing and envying, we only aggravate the circumstances. Energy of ingratitude takes effect, increases the impact of negative and makes things worse.

Sometimes losses can lead to a greater goal. Once laid off, you can decide to move to another city, and searching for interesting vacancies, you can get a dream job and live in a place, you always have been dreaming to live.

However, we lose people close to us because they might have completed their own mission. Everyone decides himself at what point of life he can leave this world. The book of Sylvia Browne "Life on The Other Side" was a huge help to me, when I lost my beloved one. I was amazed by the detailed description of my dreams in this book, therefore, it was easier to accept information and adapt to the loss.

Everything that surrounds us: envious or mentally ill people, for example, are the reflections of our own thoughts. It is very simple: if there is something unpleasant around us, we need to change ourselves, to change our attitude. If some bad memory gives no rest, it is necessary to get rid of its negative effect. And we can achieve that through the liberation, by forgiving not only offenders, but also ourselves.

No imaginary teachers, who are supposed to help if you have been bedevilled, will fix this situation, as long as offense stays inside you and while you believe in existence of harmful impact of offenders or envious people. Taking full responsibility for everything that happens in our environment, we will stop getting into such troubles.

Each of us creates his own reality. We should not blame anyone, even ourselves, as well as nobody should throw responsibility for his or her problems onto us. As soon as we are liberated from the destructive negativity, not only our life becomes different, improved, but also the life of our loved ones, because they, are our reflection. By no means we should be distressed and blame ourselves or somebody else for the current circumstances. We have to see and recognize our inner world, take responsibility for everything that happens, and understand what needs to be changed and make the necessary actions, correcting our way of thinking.

If you want to achieve something, you must begin to act. For a long period of time I thought of this as something abstract. I did not have enough courage to admit that the usual rhythm of life should be changed. There was no time to do something I really loved. I realized what "to begin to act" meant, when I dared to dream about moving to one of the southern European Countries with my whole family. This very desire pushed me to think about more important goal. I had been working as a manager, but always for somebody else, so it was time to become independent. I had to find an occupation which I could devote myself in any corner of the world, which would bring pleasure and provide a steady income.

The desire to move, to be financially independent and to have a job of my dream was an impulse, intense, strong and clear. Therefore quite soon eager to share my skills in the materialization of the desired I have started a blog about "the power of thought".

This **strong** desire forced me to master the technical side of the creation of the blog. I needed information about the art of correct writing and website optimization, so that my blog would have earning power. I mentally tuned to the thought "let all necessary information come to me", imaging myself opened to all conceivable and unthinkable possibilities. I **thirsted** for information. A week later a friend of mine called me: "Please help me sign up for the online courses about infobusiness and register you too". This was what I needed! Having had a 3- week virtual training, I was struck by the surge of information. I am tremendously grateful to everyone, who made these numerous seminars possible! This 3- week course was absolutely free, and it entered the Guinness book of records because of the number of listeners. There was a lot of really valuable and useful information, all important topics were well displayed, which guided the work of the brain in a right direction. It is real pleasure to listen to such energetic, expert and smart people. Those who are looking for information will definitely get it from these professionals and moreover will be charged with positive energy. The arbiter of this training was, literally, an aggressive call to action!

Gaining experience in writing posts for my website, I began to feel an excitement and strong desire for the bigger action. It made me want to write a book. I had made some attempts before, but something was always missing. Now I understand that I didn't have enough inspiration for this undertaking. Enthusiasm came, when I asked for it.

Having visited the museum of Henry Matisse in Nice, I suddenly realized, why we appreciate creativity so much, - because artists put the soul and the heart in their works. And love is inexhaustible power; this could be clearly seen in the works of the great master. Enthusiasm and passion were the secret of success for many creative people.

I started thinking about creation of a book more and more often. In my imagination I already saw this book published and felt love for it. By this time there was a lot of literature about thought power. People, who wrote about it, had already become famous and achieved a huge success. They had made their most daring dreams come true, and I'm only on halfway. I was full of doubts: "Here, I thought, I will attract a dream house on beautiful coast, and then I will write a book". However, the subconsciousness always said: "Write now". I suddenly thought: "What if it is my destiny, my version of the course of events? Maybe I could walk this path together with a reader?" I could not wait to share my knowledge - after all, I had already attracted health, relationship, family happiness, career growth and stable well-being. And while everything was fresh in memory, it was possible to tell at least about the essence of materialization of the thoughts to the beginners and those, who are also on halfway.

Having become inspired, I made up my mind to write "I'm Magnet". And I didn't regret! It was really fascinating to reveal something new in myself every day. The most exciting thing in the whole process of writing a book, which was new for me, was that it turned out to be both a pleasant pastime and a deep meditation. I needed this to balance my strengths and to realize my inspirations and hopes. The secret of my enthusiasm was that having written several pages, I became mentally immersed into the written lines and the information I was going to write down later. Although I was still occupied with household and my main job, these duties only gave me a chance to take a break in the creation of my book. I imagined everything, I had to describe, on a different level of consciousness where I thought by sensations and love. All this gave me the biggest pleasure, filling me with creation energy and promoting creative improvement. It was a real discovery for me! I enjoyed meditations … between the lines! I wrote with a help of my feelings which literally materialised on a paper.

Get in touch with the art more often, if you are still in search of yourself. It is your calling to leave a trace in this world and to give people some emotions, the things that can benefit. This might be making of a garden, raising kids or grandchildren, painting, writing books, look after people or animals, organization of the concerts, jewellery or fashion design, baking of the cakes etc. If you make somebody else happy doing your work, you will enjoy your activity. Calling and recognition are inseparable components. A person is truly happy, when he has a favourite occupation. And believe me, the universe will take care of the rest.

When I started to write "I'm Magnet", I felt limitless love for what I do, for the work I have found for myself. The words flew like water, as if they have been waiting for a long to come out. I have let the power of love fill my world. Entering the state of the altered consciousness, unleashing my imagination, I was opened for ideas and events, which began to appear as long-awaited guests with wide smiles on their faces. I began to understand what the expression "to start doing the things you love" meant and I had the support of the forces, which create our world.

If you have a goal, start doing things you love right now. Tell the universe firmly and lovingly: "I am ready to be carried away by something that I truly love, please, take care of the financial side!"

Read stories of successful people, watch some motivating movies, - they will certainly inspire you for your own Great Achievements.

Breakthrough or quantum leap

The book "I'm Magnet" has appeared in spring of 2012. When a quarter of the book was finished, the incredible events started happening. The universe began to show the most of it. My enthusiasm and desire to become financially independent have literally tuned my entire environment and myself to the right wave. Through the book writing I started paying attention to my life and the feeling of gratitude for everything that happens to me has strengthened. That seemed to inspire the universe to open new doors for me. Accidently, but at the same time completely naturally, as this usually happens, when a person is ready for necessary changes, the further described situation has materialized.

Talking during a friendly dinner with the neighbour about the goal of life and some possible activities, which would bring pleasure, we suddenly discovered an invisible thread that connected our minds and hearts, our visions of the future. She had years of experience of teaching in Finland and dreamed to plunge into her teaching calling, working only for herself. And I had the answers to all questions about the principles of the law of attraction and power of thought, so I probed all possible channels to share my knowledge with people. Some invisible power has connected emotions and goals of me and my neighbour and has rallied us in simple: "Let's try to do this together". We discussed the details of our cooperation and decided to organize some trainings during a year. Having gained the experience, we could defined more precisely our direction and begin independent activity.

I was not sure, there was any sense in that undertaking, and that it would be understandable to Finnish mentality. I did not know if I could handle these coming challenges and would have enough courage, but I had a vision and I strove for its manifestation in my reality.

We were actively discussing the topic of our presentation. Having planned our further steps with all responsibility, we identified the beginning of December as a time for our first show. This date, marked in the calendar, directed our work and forced us to take certain actions.

At first, we had nothing; there even was no theme for our seminar, only two beautiful notebooks and pens. But we were pushed by something. Each new meeting laid the road to the goal, making it visible, and each step provided us with incredible pleasure.

Working with materials, I was also preparing psychologically for my first public speech. It is worth mentioning that I was making the presentation on foreign language, and hadn't had any tendency to speak in front of the audience before, let alone some oratorical abilities. Therefore I did not understand how I had managed to fall in love with this business. But using regularly and successfully the principle of "ask, and it will be given to you", I have emphasized for myself the major milestones:

- I need to learn to control my voice

- I speak confidently, my story is interesting, I am not nervous

- I speak in public with a feeling of complete safety and comfort

- I love to perform in front of people, I like to share the positive energy

- I'm Magnet: Me and my voice attract the people

Have you watched Charles Jarrott's movie "The Christmas List"? A saleslady Melody Parris works in a perfume department. Once she decides to make a list of wishes and puts it into the Santa Claus's mailbox. The life of lovely Melody is full of sincere romanticism, especially after her desires start magically coming true. Same thing happened to me. Having composed my list of desires, I began opening new doors and discovering... myself. This process is quite exciting, I must admit.

We started discussing our business during the walks, where I, certainly, shared my list of desires with my neighbour. And you know what? As in that movie, I had received the desired almost instantly and "just like that". It turned out, that my future business partner was professionally teaching people to speak and to control their voices. Already after our first walk, where I had to "grimace" all the same time and actively use my voice, I noticed some tremendous changes in myself. I began to make up more complex sentences in Finnish and pronounce the words louder and more clearly. I couldn't stop talking. I began to hear myself and I liked my voice. I gained confidence that I will use my talking skills and make a brilliant official speech!

New ideas were appearing every day, the material progressed pretty rapidly. The more we worked on it, the more confident I felt. I already craved for my speech. Soon, we decided to make a trial presentation in front of each other. This was, probably, the most difficult step. The night before was full of nervousness, I could not sleep, my heart tried to jump out, I was really worried. Sleepy and tired in the morning, I summoned my will and went to take my first test.

It turned out, that we were not ready for our interactive dialogue. We had different themes and points of view, which became clear during first minutes of our test speech. I got frustrated. I wanted to forget about all this for a while. And I knew that my neighbour felt absolutely the same way. We had only two options: to give up or to find strength and re-set the tasks, which would help to achieve our goal.

And then I was tuned to the right mood... by sending love. I mentally repeated the words "I love, I love, I love" directing them to myself, to my neighbour and our joint activities. Thus, I tried to affect the energy of what was happening to us. I wanted us to understand and trust each other. Indeed, the most important thing in any successful cooperation and creation of trusting relationship is to show respect and to understand, what the other side wants. This rule works in business, family relations, in the communication with superiors or subordinates, colleagues, customers etc. The trust will not only strengthen any union, but will also create necessary conditions for the favourable progress of the business, where all participants will benefit.

Love sending, which carried positive and creative energy, has immediately affected the further course of events. The next day we were already having a constructive discussion over a cup of tea. We confessed openly to each other in our emotions and thoughts, through the gained experience we have defined some important aspects, which would contribute to a positive and creative development of our future business. We agreed upon the strategy of interactive communication during the workshop. We discussed our expectations, trust, faith in our idea, responsibility for our business's progressivity, and all this brought us to a new level, - the level, where you are appreciated and trusted. We have strengthened our creative union, gave each other confidence in the success of our joint venture.

When the remarkable day has come, strangely enough, I didn't feel any disturbance, on the contrary, there was complete harmony, as if I was waiting for a miracle. I continued to believe that I would cope with everything, would find the right words and take the audience into the world of my thoughts. I hoped that the hearts of the listeners would open the way to the world of the law of attraction.

My business partner filled in almost twenty representatives of different companies. There were pretty women sitting in front of us, among whom I immediately recognised a sceptic, a negatively minded person, professional psychiatrist and my friend, who had already been successfully using the power of thought for a long time. These individuals were clearly standing out, you could feel very powerful energy coming from them. All the others were completing the harmony, the event saturation with their openness and curiosity. An ideal atmosphere reigned there. I had a sense of safety, confidence and positive.

It was my big moment. When I studied at the Finnish university, every time the teacher asked me a question in a classroom, the whole class became silent. I had to speak in a complete silence, so that my voice echoed. I referred this to the curiosity of the Finns to my pronunciation. Many years have passed since the studies, and I've already forgotten about this experience. But, having started my presentation, I found myself in that classroom again. It was so quiet there, that I've heard an echo again. I did not even have to make any efforts to keep my voice louder. I felt it, it was pleasing and easy to control.

Our strategic plan to conduct a seminar as an interactive conversation has worked out. The audience was actively taking part in the process. Three hours ran quickly. I felt comfortable and I even had fun. I have realized my dream, did something I strived to, something that seemed impossible for me a year ago. I saw smiling faces and was able to feel the synergy of those being present, the desire of listeners to participate in what was happening. I beheld different reactions to my words and, most importantly, I was a witness of the changing way of thinking of people sitting in front of me. It was a triumph! A complete success!

I was not thinking about possible feedbacks, I was focused on the process itself. It was, certainly, more important for me to expose myself to the audience, but I did not expect that everyone will like this topic. And guess what happened next? All present have noted that the seminar was unusual and very interesting. Many have discovered a new perception of the world; some people have found useful our practical tasks. It was a real surprise for me when after the presentation one of the listeners said that my speech had a magical impact. And my friend stated enthusiastically: "You have a hypnotic style of speech, never change it, you've made people want to listen to you". My statement" I'm Magnet" helped me in this case as well!

So it took only half a year to make this idea come true. I cannot say, whether it is long or short period of time, but it is totally worth it when you make an agreement with yourself. This is a work, but moved by inspiration, which brings you pleasure and increases self-esteem. When there is a goal, absolutely everything in the universe contributes to its favourable achievement.

An amazing thing happened to me: having overcome all my fears, I have successfully coped with the task, that I had set myself. The day after the presentation one of my favourite teachers of quantum leaps, Burt Goldman, has published a question to his subscribers on his site: "If today is the first day of the rest of life, then what was yesterday?" In a split second, I realized, that yesterday I made a quantum leap, and today is the first day of my new life, with limitless possibilities, which I have opened for myself, literally, in one night. I felt that I could move mountains, there were no limitations, I have become entirely different person. I have experienced the process of an amazing quantum transition. If I clearly realize that I have enough energy and imagine the desired result and the right conditions, I can dislocate into desired reality.

All the energy that surrounds us consists of atoms, therefore the most important interactions, affecting everything in the world, are the interactions between the atoms and them constituent elementary particles. According to the quantum physics the quantum particles exist in the material form at different energy levels. Quantum physicists believe that the particles exist in more than one place at the same time, which means that people, consisting also of the particles, exist simultaneously in more than one place. Burt Goldman is one of the founders of the phenomenon, known as quantum leap, which involves quantum physics and concept of the parallel universes.

Once I was returning from a business trip and suddenly something surprising and inexplicable happened: during the flight I started feeling myself in two different planes. I realized the singularity of the whole situation only at the landing. I was in some kind of hypnotic state, thinking about my life and all events in it. I had clear memories of being in two different places at the same time and saw my reflection in the illuminators of both planes…

Relying on the idea of the infinite number of parallel universes, Burt explains that a person exists in this very moment infinite number of times.

Since we exist countless times in one moment, it means, that right now we can be a well-known politician or an actor; we can possess a yacht or have a happy family. We can be rich, but we can also go begging. We can be cruel or kind. It all depends on what kind of parallel reality we choose, what kind of life we have preferred. Burt became a famous photographer in six months. And he was already more than eighty five years old. He knew that in another dimension he was already a successful master of this craft.

You can influence your health, personal qualities, and your well-being. Create another version of yourself, imagine, for example, that you are well-known actor. Ask him how to complete the transition into alternative reality, where you are him. When the energy transfer happens, the quantum leap will contribute to the transition into another dimension.

Let me present you an example of my subsequent quantum leaps, and the quantum transition itself, directly connected with the book" I'm Magnet":

- The book "I'm Magnet" is a best-seller

- The movie "I'm Magnet" is made based on my book

- "I'm Magnet" is a MAGNET

- "I'm Magnet" provides benefits, success and good luck

- "I'm Magnet" is an incentive for the actions and contributes to the enrichment

- "I'm Magnet" is endowed with a powerful force and fulfils the desires and the dreams

- The continuation of the book "I'm Magnet" is published, and movie is filmed based on it

... One year later, as planned, me and my neighbour went different ways, independently, but supporting each other and having remained excellent friends. My personal trainings have acquired forms, and now I freely and successfully give consultations in the applying of the principles of the law of attraction, combining the power of thought, power of different energies and NLP practices.

Ground for the development of necessary circumstances

The work of the law of attraction is visible even by naked eye. Something always moves us on: the ambitions, the well-being of people close to us, the desire to be healthy. We are always looking for the way out from some situations and usually find it with the help of some unknown forces. A person, who does not practice the power of thought, begins to apply it unconsciously or, I would say, intuitively.   After all, if we look back, despite all obstacles, we continue to exist in our reality. It means that we are the creators of an instant between the past and the future. The power, that creates every moment, is inside us. Do you agree that the power, which has given birth to us, should be somewhere inside us, but not in the outside world?

We all go through life guided by intuition, and everything, we meet on our way, is not a coincidence. Every moment should be appreciated, even if it has brought us a disappointment, pain, fear or happiness. Every moment is a lesson, a sign that we are either going along the right way or something must be changed. We are creators. Life and everything happening in it are the great gifts. Excepting it, we will be able to see benefit for ourselves in any situation. If we stop taking negatively what is happening, we will open ourselves to the universe, allowing it to fulfil our desires and multiply our well-being.

So that the magnet of the law of attraction would attract something favourable, it is necessary to work on your usual perception of world. Changing the way of thinking, we influence not only our own life, but also the lives of our nearest and dearest. Having got confidence in your abilities, using the law of attraction deliberately, you will not doubt and will learn to trust. Imperceptibly the time will come, when your spouse, who did not earlier listen to your exclamations about the materialization of the desired, suddenly will exclaim joyfully: "I switch the green light on the traffic lights with a help of just one thought!" In the conversation with his or her friends he or she will suddenly begin to describe the applying the laws of the universe in your words. This will be a sign for you, that now, when nobody in your circle questions the power of the universe, you can be absolutely confident in the effect of thought. Doubts, leaving you, will leave your reflection too. The distrust of your close ones to the power of thought will disappear into thin air, and you, having gained some skills in the materialization of the desired, will become a precious teacher for someone.

The ways, of course, can be different, - the guru is able even to fly or teleport, but you can start from the small things. It is not necessary to strive for global transformation. Let's begin with the admission of the possibility, with trust, gratitude and overcoming our fears and doubts, for example.

Just a few steps will help us to get free from the obstacles, which arise on our way. Having created a strong foundation, solid staircase, we will finally get a responsible attitude to the events in our life. We will enrich ourselves, attract all the best and easily go up to the top of our dreams, materializing the wildest desires.

Each step is important in its own way, each of them will bring you near your goal:

1. Liberation or forgiveness

2. Gratitude

3. Correct formulation of the desired

4. Removing the importance

5. Faith and permission

6. Visualization and filling the desired with love

7. Inspiration, actions and choices

With further described practices, you will easily reach the summit. Meanwhile, write down your desires on the next pages. They should be solid and clear not only to you, but also to the universe. Do not afraid of excessiveness! The main thing here is, first of all, to understand, what you want.

LIST OF THE DESIRES

... for example:

- Health, family happiness

- New, modern, bright and big house on the sea shore in the calm and friendly neighbourhood

- To become a world famous photographer

- New white BMW, with a white leather interior

LIST OF THE DESIRES

Liberation or forgiveness

Once I went through a very hard period, and I knew that it was necessary to find a way out of the situation. For the sake of my family I had to bring myself back to life. I was desperately looking for a way out. That was when I got acquainted with Reiki healing practice. This appeared unexpectedly in my life and taught me how to obtain the inner peace. Each initiation has been a new breath, new force for me. I felt that every day everything around me became brighter. I have cured my inner world, my feelings, and afterwards Reiki has become an integral part of my life. It started helping me to influence the health of my entire family, relationships, situations at work, which occur in the present or happened in the past, but still have its impact on the present, as well as, the events of the future.

Reiki called me to forgive myself, all offenders and injustice. Now I am grateful to that experience, it led me to the happy, special life and understanding of everything happening in it.

Reiki has five principles. Dr. Mikao Usui, who has made Reiki energy accessible to everyone, has formulated them in the following way:

1. Just for Today, do not Worry

2. Just for Today, do not Anger

3. Just for Today, Earn your living Honestly

4. Just for Today, show Gratitude to every living thing

5. Just for Today, Honour your parents, teachers and Elders

Think about it, these rules are the main prerequisites for a happy and successful life. Being reflected in us through emotions and senses, they motivate us to find inner harmony, to feel "wings on the back" through the creation, responsibility, gratitude and love.

A happy person does not bear a grudge. We can forgive. We are created to love. And in order to come to a happy life, we should get free, clear ourselves from the destructive energies, stop letting them into our world. A person, who realizes what negative thoughts can carry, what impact they have, completely excludes them from his life with time. Such person goes to the next level, where everything becomes possible. He suddenly realizes that any pain is a resistance, and any fear prevents the natural motion. He begins appreciating everything around him, getting benefit from various events and people. A person begins to float down the stream of love and harmony.

There are the situations, when it seems that forgiveness itself is unfair. But if we wish all the best for ourselves and our loved ones, forgiveness is absolutely necessary, because each negative situation attracts another one.

In fact, it is not that difficult to forgive. You just need to take responsibility for everything that happened in the past, is happening in the present or will happen in the future. The further described method is easy and can be applied without any practice. Deep breathing is very important, it will help you to relax and to get to the level of consciousness, on which you will be able to work positively with the technique of forgiveness. Imagine how you approach your offender; picture him as a small child. He is all alone and defenceless, but at the same time he emits warmth and light, he is looking tenderly at you. Hug him, tell that you love him. The power of love will surround you, feeling tenderness for him, compassion and forgiveness, you will find love for yourself. It will be easier to let go of the situation. Even having mentally said "I love you", you already will be able to tune into the channel of love, and your space will be cleared from all negative. You will feel it, realize that there is no offense any more, only light. You will forgive.

That's another matter, when offense comes from the childhood. Perhaps, you do not remember particular situation, which has led subsequently to some problems in the adult life. In the evening, before going to sleep, when you are completely relaxed, close your eyes and return to your childhood. Look at yourself, maybe crying, maybe laughing? Embrace this child, tell him that you love him, and say that you are happy. Fill everything which surrounds you with love. You will notice that unwillingly you will start to recollect the small details of your childhood, some joyful or sad events will pop up in your memory. Together with "baby you" rejoice at the sunshine, and fill all wistful memories with love, surrounding everything by the shroud of soft light. Such journeys are funny and useful: sometimes memories bring plenty of emotions, filling our life with bright colours from the childhood. All possible sufferings of a child will slowly begin to fade, excluding, thus, their negative impact on the present or future. Always return from this journey with a pure heart, with the knowledge, that you have positively influenced your experiences in the past and your memories.

Practice the forgiveness until the total liberation or until your mind stops returning to the distributing thoughts. Sometimes I simply mentally repeat "I love, I love, I love". The strength of these words is just as powerful as love itself. The energy of the word "love" is equivalent to the feeling of love, if your mind is pure, and your intentions are sincere. If at first it is difficult for you to fill the offenders or situations with the love in the present or in the past, you can always appeal to the Prayer. Indeed, using any positive energy with miraculous power, whether it is energy of Love, Reiki or Prayer, it is possible to affect any situation, including our inner state. They all have the same source of harmony and light in them. Maybe someone will just find prayers easier and more understandable to use. If you still experience some difficulties directing the words of the prayer to the circumstances or people, ask the saints for help, to correct the situation, to give you strength to tune into the forgiveness.

Offences, suffering are a kind of manipulation, the demonstration, that life is unfair. You can live, revelling in self-pity, or, in spite of all the troubles, start a new life, full of joy and happiness.

Do not lose temper with your child. If you were wrong or even if you were right, but have shouted at him, hug this little person, ask him to forgive you for all negative, that you have brought into the situation. The child will learn to forgive and will not get used to take offense at the world. If there is love, there is no place for resentments. Thus, no insults will have any negative consequences in his adult life.

Do not have grudge against your soul mate. Sincere relationships will never run out, if our ego, our points of view and our ignorance do not poison them.

Forgiveness is an integral part of the attraction of the desired. Forgiveness allows cleaning up the blockings, which have their roots in our past. Resentment in the heart, both internally and externally, seriously disrupts the energy and does not let the universe create an improved reality. So we cannot fully focus on the materialization of desires. Fortunately, as soon as we recognize the need of forgiving, everything else is obtained easily.

A habit of blaming others for your problems has negative impact on the events in your life. One injustice after another continues to destroy our peaceful existence. Make a little effort to forgive, let go, and you will be completely liberated from the negative and destructive energies.

One of my best friends was so fascinated by the power of the thought, that it inspired her to put her emotions on paper. Suddenly she discovered that, having appealed with a help of the diary to the situations of her childhood, she has felt a great relief and freedom. This is one of the great ways to experience the forgiveness: write a letter to your offender, explaining that you are no longer angry at him, that you wish him love and happiness. When you finish, you can simply throw your appeal out.

Make sure that you also do not have grudge against God or the universe. Many people believe by mistake that they are victims of some circumstances, which prevent them from the achievement of the goals and put the obstacles on their way to happiness and prosperity. Having consciously forgiven the universe, you will liberate a huge amount of creative and constructive energy.

Forgive yourself and do not ever blame yourself. Remember that every experience is an integral part of the learning process and personal growth, it helps you to approach your goal.

Do not focus on past mistakes and problems, be peaceful. After all, everything, that happened, has already passed away, and there is an exciting life ahead of you. Create the right conditions for the happy transformation!

Gratitude

There is an old Russian saying: "We know not what is good until we have lost it". We do not know, what is good, because we are not thankful for it. The way to the Heart lies through the Gratitude.

You should feel a deep gratitude to the grandmother, who spends time with your child; to the employer for the stability, he gives you and you don't spend tedious time sitting at home; to the husband for his love; to the child just for the fact that he is in your life; to the roof over your head. We send light energy, we build a bridge, we thank the environment, installing kindness and strength around us, **we give good to others**. In response, the universe does the same: gives good to us, to our environment, multiplying the value of what we value and for what we are thankful.

Gratitude must come from the heart. It must be notable both for us and for everything and everyone that creates our reality. Nobody is obliged to us for anything. Grandmother will always respond with the pleasure to your request to spend time with your child, if she feels your appreciation. Not simple "thanks", but deep gratitude and your love, will make her feel happy and useful.

If you do good things for someone, your thoughts must be pure and sincere, and then in exchange you will get gratitude. As they say: "Enough is as good as a feast". This proverb has two meanings. When we expect good in response to our good deeds, the forces of equilibrium interfere into the process. The good we do is not sincere and unselfish, if we expect some kind of attention to us.

Only sincere, "good giving" behaviour will be taken with the real gratitude.

When gratitude comes from the heart, you are happy, and therefore, you can see a benefit absolutely in everything. But if you complain about your boss, - he feels this through the energy, you send him by your thoughts. You become ungrateful in his mind. On the contrary, if you ask him for advice, or send him love, he will feel your appreciation. It will unite you and take you to the advanced level of communication, where you will solve problems constructively. Gratitude is one of the powerful means to change your life.

Thank the universe for every moment, the sun for the light and warmth, the nature for the beauty, the rain for the memories. Waking up in the morning, do not jump out of the bed, stay and stretch at least for half a minute, always with a smile. Feel gratitude for the new day. Mentally repeat times: "I'm Magnet", with a feeling, that you attract only good events.

Hug your loved ones more often, showing that you are grateful to them for the fact that there they are in your life. Feel free to say them about this aloud. I remember the surprise on a pretty little face of my dear daughter, when I said to her for the first time: "Thank you for being in my life". "Mom, why do you say so, I have been in your life for a long period of time!" – She wondered. "Well, I said, I'm just very happy, that I have you". Feeling so much love and gratitude, your kids will never get sick, and even if they get ill, then they will recover quicker because of your embraces.

Gratitude is your weapon or tool, as you want. With gratitude, you can attract necessary circumstances.

Thank God, thank the universe for the fact that you are healthy, even when you are sick, for the fact that peace and love are in your house, even if you are quarrelling with your husband every day, for the fact that your boss gives you bonuses, even if it seems that you do not have any points of contact. Be grateful for all the money you get, even if you have no idea, where can they come from. Be the grateful for the bills, coming by mail. Thank even the driver of the passing car that has splashed you up. Your emotional front will not be disrupted, you will break the chain of negative circumstances and, quite likely, the situation itself will lead you to some favourable outcome. Maybe, the driver of this car is an official, who can help you sign all necessary papers in some bureau or, what is more interesting, he might be your future spouse.

Gratitude attracts everything you have dreamed about, it improves relationships, makes us more confident, attracts people to us and eliminates negative thinking. Gratitude offers opportunities, teaches us to appreciate not really pleasant situations, thus moving us forward to favourable circumstances, developing our natural state of happiness, which is so necessary for the law of attraction. Gratitude removes obstacles. And no matter what is happening in your life right now, be grateful! Think about the benefits you will get from the current situation, forget about everything bad or unfair. Practice the power of gratitude in your family and with your friends. Discuss with them what happened today and what you are grateful for.

Remember, a person is happy not when he has everything, but when he is grateful for what he has. Your life will become truly fabulous, when you bring the power of gratitude in it:

* Be grateful

- Use good, positive words

- Choose positive thoughts and feelings

- Appreciate yourself

- Focus on what you appreciate

Try to write here the list of the things you are grateful for. It is not that difficult to identify the pleasant moments in your life:

- Thanks for the bright thoughts

- Thanks for my clever daughter

- Thanks for being healthy

- Thanks for the happiness of my family

- Thanks for the golden autumn

- Thanks for the best colleagues

- Thanks for the clean house

- Thanks for the attentive spouse

- Thanks for…

When you re-read your list, you thereby return again and again to what you have. You learn to appreciate life and to remember that there always is a place for the gratitude. You open your heart to the universe. Paying attention to something you value, you will notice that your power of gratitude becomes stronger, and the quality of your life improves.

When I go jogging sometimes the sky is covered with thick clouds, but there is always a ray of light breaking through, and I address to it with the words:

-Sweetie, you are so brave trying to make a way through the clouds, thank you for that!

Gratitude to the sun ray will suddenly draw the clouds apart, the sky begins to lighten, and by the end of my run it is almost clear. Well, the same is in life. We may have not much, but endowed with gratitude, it begins to multiply. And it doesn't matter, whether this concerns your health, your bank account or your relationship. Clouds dissipate, when we are grateful.

Under any circumstances, believe me, you can always find something you can be grateful for. Thank sincerely and from your heart. Make it a habit to thank everything and everyone around you from the early morning: while washing, making breakfast or on the way to work. A person, who meets new day with gratitude, is automatically tuned to the desired frequency, to the harmony with the environment. And believe me, when you are in harmony with yourself, nothing bad can happen to you.

Correct formulation of the desired

The materialization of the desired depends on how we shape it, by what thoughts, words, feelings and emotions. The purer our intentions are, the more favourable environment becomes, the faster our desires are fulfilled, and the easier it gets to use the law of attraction.

Right words and thoughts

In a month I suddenly saw 1000 € on my bank account, which I had attracted by the power of thought. It made me want to pay off the old debt as soon as possible. At that moment it already reached 7000 €. I marked for myself a period of half a year and having counted how much per month I need to pay back, I started imagining the necessary income, not forgetting about the desired balance of 1000 € that had always remain on my account. I also dreamed to travel a lot, so I needed some extra savings too. First of all, the phrase "I repay the debt" I have replaced by "I'm giving 7000 € to the bank". The word "debt" does not carry positive associations. The phrase "I repay a debt" completely repelled me, so I couldn't tune to the right mood. I found it easier to imagine that I bring to the bank some 7000 €, divided into 6 months. It took me some time, two or three months, to get used to the idea that it was possible. But afterwards everything went smoothly: paying a greater amount of money every month (now with a feeling of happiness), I suddenly began to notice that there was already more than 1000 € on my account! That was money for our holidays. All my actions, thoughts and emotions I filled with love. I can only imagine what was going on with the bankers. I think, they gleefully wondered, where all that love and gratitude were coming from. And the banks of Finland, I am sure, were prospering, because of so many positive emotions "invested" in them.

It is important to replace the words and phrases that carry negative associations with the positive assumption of the course of the events. If you come to your boss asking to raise a salary, but subconsciously repeat dissatisfied "I do not care about you", then the salary will not be increased. Designate that amount of money that you expect to get, imagine the happy face of your boss, mentally give him a present before the meeting, something very-very beautiful, for example, a new yacht gleaming in the sun. The music is playing on its deck, beautiful couples are dancing. Create the bridge between you and your boss, our thoughts are material! Smile at him, repeat mentally: "I love, I love, I love". After that your salary will be raised, the company's business will improve, your boss will be happy and in love with his or her spouse, and you will get a prize. Do not forget to thank the universe for all of this. Later you can go with your boss and his family for a ride on that yacht, you have been picturing, and that has materialized.

If you want to get well quickly, do not complain about your health, tell everyone that you are already getting better. If I get ill (which happens rarely), I report to the work, always beginning my mail with: "today I will stay at home to get better".

If you do not have infinite riches yet, but you strive to it, say: "I am not rich yet, but I'm already on my way to the wealth".

Speaking with a child, gently demonstrate your respect for him, do not use the words that cause negative emotions or associations. Instead of "come on, hurry up, we will be late because of you", say: "please, get dressed, so that we could do all planned things". If it is hard for your child to learn foreign languages, direct his or her thoughts to the idea that, in reality it is easy, let him repeat: "I like to learn French", for example.

Once, I got under the flash of the traffic police camera. I immediately convinced myself that I drove according to the rules and, even if I had exceeded the speed a little, the registration number of my car was blurry and blown out on the picture. In addition to that I imagined myself invisible: I was not there, so there was no violation and no police with a camera.

Particle" not" and worries

Only in case of desperation or very strong desire the particle "not" might work. "I'm not afraid" - can the businessman repeat, trying to promote the work of his company and to attract enough customers. "I am not sick" - a person repeats with burning chest, desperately seeking to get healthy.

When we state our intentions, the universe does not understand particle "not". If we wish "I have no debt", then this is equivalent to "I have a debt". "I will not be fired" for the universe sounds like "I will be fired" and so on.

Do not worry about your child, trust the school, the kindergarten, the universe, his friends, the roads, the cars. Everything around him creates a favourable environment and complete safety. Someone said to me once: "It is easy to say "do not worry"". But I would like to make a point: it is easier to trust, since this is the only way we can protect ourselves and our close ones, not creating anything negative by our worries. Trust the universe, replace the intentions by correct expressions, without particle "not", and let them evoke only positive emotions.

I'm a mother, and I know, that it is natural to worry about a child. But I do not allow myself to doubt, I only let myself think that everything is all right with my child. Because this is the only way I can affect his safety or favourable outcome of some situation, in which he has found himself. Worrying and caring are two different things. I trust my child and the universe, I trust God and my invisible helpers. I have found huge help in Reiki, namely, protection attunement. Almost every day I ask St. Michael the Archangel to let me be his mediator and to give the ray of protection to my child. I mentally surround my child, the school, the road, the house by soft white light. And I send this protection not only to the child, but also to the whole family and myself. At the end of each attunement I thank St. Michael. You can also appeal to him or to any other saint, with whom you feel the connection. You will sense that you and everyone you love are protected by his presence in your life.

All, who practice the materialization of thoughts, advise not to watch and not to read the news. Now, when I am passionate about writing a book, I have almost no time to watch TV. If we see the something bad happening on our planet on the news, we automatically exclaim: "It's horrible!", thereby not helping people, who have faced a tragedy, but only worsening circumstances. Taking the experience of other people personally, we attract negative situations to ourselves. We bring this power of trouble into our reality, which will be equal in proportion to the strength of our response. The phrase "What a horror!" may attract, for example, misunderstanding or quarrels, since our energy balance is disrupted. I do not encourage you to be indifferent, but to use the creative practice in any cases. Instead of the pitiful sympathy, which is not carrying anything positive in itself, you are able to influence favourably the situation or the emotional level of people by sending love. This will give them strength and balance or facilitate the creation of better conditions and circumstances. In fact, the need of love is the basis of human existence.

I want to tell you about one example from my own life, related to the TV news. There were only few people, with whom I was able to share this, but, I think, this example was convincing enough for those, who know this story. Once there was a strip of news on TV about the women, who had been used as sexual slaves against their will. I got very disturbed when I saw that news flash. "Can I help them somehow?" - I was asking myself. I felt the urge to surround them with energy of love as much as possible. In such cases, probably others pray for suffering people, which undoubtedly can help. I used the powerful force of love and, as my heart prompted to me, I started desperately direct the words "I love, I love, I love" to the women seeking salvation. I surrounded them with light coming from my heart, filled the reasons, which had led them to that challenge. And after couple of days I heard on the news: "Service X has set free about 3000 female slaves that had been captured for a long time..." I could not describe my feelings at that moment! Splash of the emotions of all kind with tears and wild happiness!

Since then, having heard about the tragedy somewhere, even about the drug addicts, I send love. I believe that this helps people.

New epidemics, as it seems to me, are far-fetched, usually they are made up to provoke fear and panic among people. Therefore, I would advise you to watch TV and to read newspapers as little as possible in order not to create negative vibrations and not to let the consequences of these events into your life. Do not "try on" the bad news, which do not always relate to you, send love instead.

Trust the universe, do not worry about anything. The universe will justify your trust through the power of love. It will do anything for you. Focus on the concrete result, filled with love. Right doctor will be found and will cure someone you love, relationship will get to a better level, and bills will be paid. But money - money is an energy, there is no need to wonder where it comes from, thus questioning the work of the universe. Money appears, when the direction for it is indicated.

Do not be afraid of responsibility, do not tear your hair exclaiming: "How to fix it all? Isn't it too late? " It is never not late, my dear readers! Any positive thought and the power of love are million times stronger than any negative thought or grievances! Just keep this in mind and, if necessary, say mentally: "I love, I love, I love". This resets the situation and all negative impacts to zero.

Train your spirit, your inner power. Thoughts and emotions do not have limitations, but they are manageable, and with their help we can even create the events exceeding all our expectations. Our fears do not have physical form, but they are always the main obstacle on the way to the achievement of the goals. When the fear seizes us, we are not able to move forward, but indeed, each of us has all the cards of fate in our hands.

Older people, who have huge life experience, say that most of all they regret only about one thing in their life - the time spent on the unjustified fears and worries. World is considerably bigger than we are used to think. In any situation it is necessary to rise, gather the courage and make a step towards your dream.

Affirmations

Constantly repeating the same phrase or statement, we get used to it and are starting to believe, that everything we say is true. The faith is a sensation, clear enough for the universe, so it urgently begins the work on the materialization of our thoughts and desires.

Try it yourself and make your own affirmations begin with "I'm Magnet…", for example:

- I'm Magnet for the successful people that bring confidence, entrepreneurial spirit, knowledge and money into my life

- I'm Magnet for the new ideas

- I'm Magnet for…

- My wallet is a magnet for…

- I'm Magnet for the happy family relationships

I was so happy to hear suddenly during my husband's conversation with his friends, that I am his talisman. The most interesting thing is that I believe in it. And the more I believe in it, the more I feel myself bringing happiness and even success to the others. Perhaps, the development of personal magnetism, the self-energy, gained during the actions, which move me to the dream, suddenly have created a vacuum of happiness and love around me. My loved ones are in this vacuum too and they feel it. My beloved husband feels so good with me, that he sees me as a talisman bringing him luck. It is an amazing affirmation for those, who want to build a fine relationship with his or her love, isn't it?

- I'm a talisman for my husband/ my wife

If a child does not like reading, first of all begin from yourself. Use, for example, the affirmation: "My child loves to read, he reads one book after another". Believe that it will be so, feel faith in this inside you. Print the words "I read well and I like to read" and hang them in the child's room on a prominent place. You can paint something together with your child on this affirmation list. And every time the child will read these words, ask him to decorate the inscription with a sticker. Make this fun. Update your affirmations together with your child by adding, for example:

- I'm lucky

- I'm the minion of fortune

You can do the same with the colleagues at work: replace your outrage because of some misunderstanding by:

- I have excellent relations with my colleagues

- We have a wonderful atmosphere at work

- My colleagues are always happy to help me

The constant repetition of the phrase "I am healthy" will lead to the complete recovery: all necessary resources and doctors will be found, or a miracle will happen. The words "He is mine, he is mine" may result in a marriage.

There is an excellent affirmation in the wilds of the Internet: "The cosmic abundance brings a huge flow of money into my life". It should be pronounced or written 54 times each day, with joy and gratitude.

A repetition of "thank you for…" in the beginning of the affirmations will attract the required amount of money, for example: "thanks for 2000 €".

In the present

Draw the coordinate system on a sheet of paper. Put a pencil between the lines; mark a few points on it in mind. Each point is an individual situation today. Such point on the pencil can be related to the family, the work, the children and your vision about the materialization of the desired. Now imagine this coordinate system in the space around you. Where will your pen be located? And what about the points, where are they? These are versions of your life, as well as scenarios of the course of events in your parallel realities here and now. Let yourself look in the parallel, where your life is improved. You have everything you want, - take a picture of this in your mind. Starting from today, imagine this picture; thank God, the universe, the Supreme Mind for the dreams materialized in your life and the desired circumstances in the present.

There is a great and effective technique of golden images in the Silva Method (developed by José Silva). Imagine a blue frame and place in it a situation, which you want to change or to exclude from your life. Into the white frame put the situation you would like to have. For example, in order to gather courage and to begin to train people, to make your speech more confident and perform in front of a large audience, you should place an image of you or your fears into the blue frame. In the lower left corner of the blue frame you will place a small white frame, in which the audience is listening to you spellbound, applauds, and congratulates you on your success.

Picture in the white frame must remain small, imperceptible, and black and white. Swap the pictures. Now the image, where you are not confident, placed earlier into the blue frame, must be located in right lower corner of the image in the white frame. Then create a golden image. Everything that is in the white frame, we enlarge and add some colours to make the picture clear and bright. Everything in the blue frame, we decrease, make an image in it fuzzy and black and white. This is due to the fact that the right side corresponds to the past, and the left to the future. Thus, we shift the perception, we change our usual emotions and beliefs, create a comfortable and useful thought forms. The transformation of our consciousness happens.

The technique of golden images can be used both in your personal situations and concerning your environment. If you want to help a loved one, for example, to get rid of his or her bad habits, you should create a bright and colourful image, where he has healthy life style. Put this image into the enlarged white frame, and undesirable picture of him or her having bad habits put into the small blue frame in the right lower corner.

Many people tend to avoid what is happening right now. Instead of changing the present moment, they are in a constant striving for being someone they must be, in their opinion, or whom they want to be. Speaking once with a friend of mine about the life among the foreigners I let myself notice that her dissatisfaction with the culture of the country, in which she was living, will be absolutely the same in another country, where she was dreaming to move. It is completely wrong to think that the happiness can be found, if an economic situation, relationship, or a situation at work is different. The law of attraction must be used in this very moment, right here and right now. Discomfort in the present never will pass away, until re-evaluation and acceptance of the present moment has happened. I use a fairly simple method to rebuild my way of thinking: when some dubious thought suddenly arises in my mind I just turn it off, light goes out, and then I replace it with any useful thought: "I'm the sun", "everything will come itself", "I'm the owner of my dream house", "thank you", "I love" and so on.

The following exercise will help to understand the nature of visualization "in the present". Instead of imagining someone's beautiful body or dreaming about your perfect shape, but in the future, mentally transfer into the zone of your abdomen and slightly tighten the muscles. Feeling the work of your body in the present, imagine a thin waist, concentrate on it. The more you consciously work on your waist, the faster its elastic forms will begin to acquire. You pay attention to it in the present, so the dominant thoughts contribute to the desired forming of your waistline right now. Thus, the visualization of a dream house in the present can be, for example, combined with any slight physical action, which will help to perceive the present moment: slightly squeeze your earlobe with two fingers or pinch yourself a little. Let your house be in the mountains. The extraordinary breath-taking beauty surrounds you, happiness and appreciation are overflowing your heart, and mountain air excites your mind. You meet sunrise, you hear the bells of the sheep, grazing in a pasture. Keep this sense of the present, by nipping, tapping, stroking, - you can choose any method suitable for you.

When we practice awareness of the present moment, we see the models of our thoughts. And, having consciously changed them, we reach the energy balance with our desires or the desired circumstances, instead of fighting which is more customary for us. We live at the different levels of consciousness, but we can intentionally switch to the higher level.

Vigilance and wakefulness in the present will make it possible to be in harmony with the Source, to develop a natural feeling of joy and happiness. Let's delve into our inner world and our natural power, let's feel the moment of present. Close your eyes and imagine energy in the form of a sphere inside you, slowly enjoy the warmth and peace that it emits. Turn off all your memories, your life experience, your emotions and thoughts. Enjoy the love that is within you. Imagine that the energy of the sphere becomes a bright light and spreads throughout the body. Imagine how the light breaks through the skin and fills everything around you, and then, all other layers of your world. You are the priceless miracle of the universe and the creator of your own life. Thank for the fact that you have been given an earthy incarnation, for your thoughts and your inner light that create your environment. Be grateful for everything you have and are going to get... in the present. Feel this moment. Return to this beautiful practice even when you are worried or when you need to gather your inner power. You will not only create a harmony around yourself, but also increase your beneficial effect on the world surrounding you. I use this method as well, when I feel the need of grounding, of a certain discharge of the speeds, when there is a need for a little cooling off in anticipation of the future events, to plunge into the blissful state of present moment.

It is amazing, how the business starts going up, the dreams begin to manifest in your reality, when you switch your attention to the moment of "here and now", being grateful for everything.

Everything, created by us, is created at the present moment. We pay attention to our desires now, in the present, and the law of attraction materializes our dreams now, in the present.

With the benefit for all

How many times have I heard, that it is necessary to be accurate with the wishes, because they will come true! Absurd, but I, certainly, understand what people mean. Those say this, who do not have habit to tune to the favourable final result: **with the benefit for all.** Namely inner confidence that everything will be fine for all participants is a guarantee of the safe realization of your intention. "With the benefit for all" will train you to believe in the positive outcome and create all necessary conditions to ensure that each participant of the on-going materialization, including yourself, would benefit from the manifestation of your desires.

To each "I want" add "with the benefit for all", and you will go through the right development of events. Everything that corresponds to your vibrations will come to you miraculously. But if something is not moving forward, let it go, only something beneficial to everyone around you, can become yours.

Once having forgotten about this rule, I recall this every time when I make a wish. Another comical situation, but is worth mentioning, as a true life example. When my baby was already nine months old, I decided to return to podium, to the fashion shows. The invitation came suddenly, so I had to get into shape quickly. Taking advantage of the power of thought, I decided to lose five kilograms within a night. Well, that night turned out to be something! The "Malaise" was so extreme that in the morning almost five kilograms were lost. But, to my regret, that evening I was not able to join the fashion show.

"Disappear with the benefit for all" - this phrase (in my mind only, of course) helped me every time somebody was teasing me at work. Three such cases happened to me, and this method has worked each time and without difficulty. After a couple of months I, together with those individuals, rejoiced over their career take-off: new company, the bigger salary, new wonderful boss and so on. But I must say that together with these cases such kind of people has completely disappeared from my life, and I didn't have to use this technique any more.

Visualizing the next stage of my life, I do not think, who from the people close to me will accept my manifested desires or what place they will take in them, I simply remember that they will benefit of all happening to me.

If you want to lose weight, then enjoy the process, when you eat, slowly and with a pleasure chew food repeating: "Everything brings benefit, my metabolism is working wonderfully". Imagine your slender figure. Thank your organism and your body for the fact that they obey you.

Everything that you do, everything is for the benefit! With this in mind, even the water will become healing, and the chocolate eaten at night will bring an ideal sleep and metabolism. After all, all depends on your beliefs: "I eat and become slim, everything is for the benefit" – is an outstanding intention, isn't it? But you have to believe in this calmly and confidently, without any doubts. In any case, I encourage each of you to the proper nutrition, but if you like to pamper yourself, never think of some unwanted consequences that it would entail. After all, the thought is material.

Complete now your wish list above, adding to each intention: "with the benefit for all".

Removing the importance

Allow yourself to have whatever you want. Perhaps, now, because of certain fears and prejudices you are unable to attract, for example, a private plane. Subconsciously you can afford it but your consciousness blocks the free flow of the energy in the process of visualization, and some doubts arise: "How will I get it?" Begin with the new white cabriolet, for example. Having attracted the cabriolet, you will allow yourself to dream about your own aircraft. It is always necessary to have bigger dreams, but for some people even a bicycle is a big dream. Therefore, in order to train your mind, to gain an experience, I would advise you to begin with more earthy desires.

1000 € was an amount that I consciously and subconsciously could afford at that moment to bring into my life. Now this amount has increased and I can allow it on all emotional levels. Begin from something small, let it be 100 € for a start, but after this money suddenly will appear "out of nowhere", you will realize that it doesn't matter how many zeros are in the asked sum.

Vadim Zeland, the author of the book "Reality transferring", gives a clear definition of the created imbalance of energy. If we attach a great value to something, we idealize our dream, creating an excessive potential. The power of balance becomes disrupted, but, according to the principles of the law of attraction, there should always be a harmony in the universe for a favourable outcome of a situation. A certain mechanism initiates the forces directed towards the liquidation of the imbalance, rather than realization of our dream.

If we boast of something, demonstrate our superiority, the power of balance takes effect, lowering that eagerness that we bring into the situation. We face the lack of understanding, interpreting it as envy.

The more excessive self-confidence we have, the more likely we face disappointment. If you have been promised a salary raise and you tell about this all your colleagues with a sense of superfluous superiority, do not expect the salary to be really increased. The power of balance will "blunt" the course of events in this case.

When we face troubles, they are always followed by something nice: a rainbow after a storm, light at the end of the tunnel, success after failure and so on.

If you feel confident doing what you do, show your good sense in the realization of your idea. Then you will find understanding, help and approval. Instead of giving importance to your desire or to the problem, you just need an INTENTION to solve it or to implement.

Always complete what you have planned and do not be superfluously talkative. Keep your own energy and the energy of your dream. When you have almost achieved it, you will notice a special excitement, I would say, the energy of exciting anticipation. This is an incomparable feeling, when it has been accumulated and not shared with others. Do not waste this energy in vain, but direct it towards the success of your goal. This will be much more useful. You should make an impression on other people by your achievements, rather than stories about something you are aiming for.

Treat your desires with indifference, even the most cherished. It is important to keep the peace in mind, to have a childlike frankness, enjoy every day and trust the universe, rejecting all doubts. If you let the situation go, the inner confidence will come and lead you to the desired chain of the favourable events on your way to the goal. Keep calm and inner balance, even if you share your successes, share it with respect. Have a realistic approach to the idea so that you would have enough energy to affect favourably the materialization of the desires.

When I have decided myself, what kind of job I want, what position and in what city, I have written my desire on the self-made paper airplane and let it out of my car window while driving along the highway. That action helped me to get free from the importance of the desire and all unnecessary doubts: my order has been sent. In fact we get what we request, when we are sincere and are not dependant on our goal.

If you dream to get pregnant and you spend all your energy on the fulfilment of this dream, saying to yourself that a child is the meaning of your life, you create, thus, an excess potential. The removal of importance from conception and birth, oddly enough, begins from the humble acceptance, that you cannot have children. It is important to admit the infertility and to feel your fears in order to perceive the cause and correct it. Intention cannot be pure and sincere, as long as you cling to the resistance to the infertility. Only having accepted the present moment, having healed your inner world, you can begin to work with the intention to have a baby. Wrap yourself up with a state of happiness and love right now.

Point the light of love on your emotional state, your past mistakes. Take away the responsibility for your happiness from the future child. Let him appear in your life and let him know that he will have his own life. He would not have to justify the requirement of his parents to make them happy. Repeat every day, that you are pregnant, you are healthy. Children appear three months prior to conception, you will feel it. The child might be already near you, but you are not letting him in by your excessive resistance to the problem itself. Send him a sincere love, let him know that he would be save with you.

Faith and permission

My dear Rhonda Byrne in her book "The Power" gives, in my opinion, the easiest example which helps both to remove the importance from the intention, and to afford having unusually large scale of the desired. Imagine your large modern dream house on a sea shore as a small point. Perceiving the desired house as a point, we remove an attachment to the goal, thus, giving the universe so called the freedom for the creation. The universe does not care whether you want a piece of delicious cake or a luxury house! Once you understand this, even a private plane will be possible to attract, if needed.

Should we believe in the power of thought? In the beginning I also asked myself this question, and my friend once told me: "You have taken over the control of the power of thought, so it works for you". I think, for those who practice it the question "to believe or not to believe" it is not relevant. But it is worthwhile to raise this theme here. The power of thought works always, no matter if we believe in it or not. But we really can use it consciously. My greatest teacher in the development of this faith is my daughter. When she was a little girl, she constantly had an earache. Once when she got ill for the third time I decided to stop doubting that miracles are possible and to focus on a thought, that everything will be over and this problem will never bother us again, if I put my hands on her ears. The most important thing is to formulate the intention correctly. If I held my hands with a thought "This can be cured only by antibiotics", nothing would work out. Moreover, the fears would materialize, and the recovery wouldn't be possible without some serious medication. I had to affect the health of my child by the power of thought, it was my duty as a mother and I had to gain the faith in it. I took responsibility for the welfare of my daughter. With a help of right mood and treatment, my child has recovered.

Instead of scrolling through the versions of "not getting" something, we should search for all possible favourable outcomes. Some people just can't stop thinking about the failure and to let go the desired, constantly asking themselves: "Where will I get a million for my dream house?" While there are so many scenarios: the relatives can sent some money, the envelope with a cash can fall down from the sky, you can get a bonus at work or win a lottery, the construction company may compensate the damage from building the store near your house and so on. Enjoy the moment, do things you love, play more with the kids, go for a walk, run, laugh, dance, thus proving to the universe, that you trust it. Do not cling to the desires, be happy today, and then the universe will notice your happiness and multiply it!

There is always something happening in your environment. By learning to read the signs, to point your actions or thoughts in a right direction, you can achieve a great success. Life is a game, you should approach it easily and with humour, that is how we will create harmony and the right soil for our garden of desires.

Get used to believe in the execution of your wishes and let the universe make them true, without any questions like "how?" In the course of time this will become a habit, and you will achieve your goals easily and freely.

Visualization and filling the desired with love

Visualization is considered as an extremely effective tool for healing. It is proven that it can help to relieve pain, to accelerate the healing process, to relieve stress, anxiety, tension. Unfortunately, the majority of the images that pop-up in our minds do more harm, than good, since the most common type of imagination is wrapped by worries and negative expectations. In reality, all worries exist only in our imagination, and, if we learn "to filter" our emotions, leaving only positive, we will be able to change both our physiology and the world around us.

Many athletes use visualization techniques as a part of the trainings or competitions. They develop a competitive advantage, expand their consciousness, a heightened sense of confidence and success. Visualization is a rehearsal of upcoming events. And waiting is a prophecy.

A family friend, who has been trained in a well-known tennis academy, shared with me an instructive example from the life of the athletes: if a player is upset for more than ten seconds, he becomes an outcast. Athletes use visualization technique to programme the outcome of training or match, as though, visiting the future events. Imagining the details, they also inflate future events with needed emotions, joy of victory. Same images repeated create an experience of achievements in the mind of an athlete, thus giving him confidence in his abilities at the emotional level. It is clear that the discussions about possible losses are not acceptable. Only endurance and determination are welcomed among the athletes.

Using the visualization technique properly, you can clearly see a positive image in the smallest details. Imagine yourself running, you are strong and fast, feel your healthy mind. Your brain will interpret imaginary run as a real motion and will allow your subconscious mind to think that you are performing this action with the ease, without feeling stress or fatigue. Your visualization will influence the nervous system and the same muscles as in real running will be used.

With a proper visualization it is possible to improve the quality of life, to attract success and prosperity, to materialize the desires. This technique can change the circumstances and conditions, influence the events and the situations, attract a job, people, health, money, cars, yachts, houses, journeys. Visualizing a certain situation or event, imagining a dream car or a house, we attract all this into our life, because we are acting in the field of our magnetism.

The process of visualization is similar to the state of dreaming, when we, being distracted from everyday life, dive into the favourable environment, where we mentally scroll the certain event or imagine certain object, for example, a new car. This technique of materialization is natural and you can successfully use it in the daily routine. And again, the more we are focused on the desire, the faster it is converted in our physical world. To prevent destructive fears and doubts disturbing the creative process of the universe, we can take advantage of any positive energy. We can satiate all happening with love.

Standing in line or waiting for a bus, visualize how one more cash desk is opened or suddenly another bus arrives (it doesn't matter where it will come from). Fill this desire with love by sending the light energy to the desired result. Practice visualization in all situations, even when you need to take up the time usefully. At work I often visualize that the new complex task will be accomplished easily or some specialists will appear and help me to resolve this issue. At the same time, I mentally repeat: "I love, I love, I love" and, certainly, I use the power of gratitude.

Each new successful experience will enhance your skills both in the materialization and in the use of the power of love.

According to Indian philosophy, world is what we think about it. Take a look at the current conditions, relationship; do you see the connection between your usual perception of the world and the circumstances? By changing our thoughts and means we create a new improved reality. What we are changing is not material; we only change the thoughts that form our world. And love is an all-consuming, all adjusting substance that can open every door. Where is love, there is balance.

I like to imagine how I wander barefoot around a sandy beach, looking at the turquoise water and at the sun rays playing on it. I love to stand, enjoying the breeze from the sea. I am wearing a long fluttering sea-green dress. I like to sit and draw on the sand. I adore sea, my love to it is unconditional. What do you love? Imagine yourself in the mountains, in the woods or on your private yacht.

Some people believe that visualization is easier to practice in bed in the morning or at night before going to sleep. However, if you are experienced in the use of this technique, you can apply visualization during the day, spending just a few minutes on it.

Take a look at the sky and try to imagine a cloud in a shape of heart. Capture this image and slowly let it disappear. Repeat this several times, until the visualization of a sharp picture becomes an easy and natural process. The second option is to come mentally to the mirror and examine well your reflection in it, first of all your face. Repeat this, until you are able to hold the reflection in order to examine it well. Then look at your hands and at your body. Get used to the images in your mind. Each time your imagination will be enriched, and with it your ability to focus the attention on the visualized object. Sending love to your reflection, you will feel yourself better, your mood will be improved. Visualizing yourself slim and healthy, successful and confident, you will thus begin to attract these states or qualities, and you will increase your energy and your magnetism.

Let's attract together something more familiar. Imagine an apple on your work table or a new suit. Add to the visualization the smell and the taste of a juicy apple or the sense of the material of your suit. Add an action or a motion to make the picture vivid. Now flavour your desire with some emotions: you like the smell and the taste of the apple (you love apples!), while in the suit you feel irresistible (you love yourself and the beautiful things!). Your wish must have a bright image, visible and tangible, and emotions will fill it with their life-giving energy and make it real.

When my child attended a kindergarten, and I had to hurry through the traffic jams to pick him home in time, I started imaging how much time I wanted to spend on the way to the kindergarten. After that I drove up to the doors exactly at 16.30 I, having spent only half an hour on a road instead of usual one hour and a half. My child grew up, and I do not have problems with traffic jams anymore, but since then I always use this visualization, for example when I need to be in time at some important meeting. As you see, the pre-specified time or date of the desire fulfilment is very important.

Let's say you decided to buy an apartment. Search the photos of a property you like in the Internet or in the magazines. Let your moving be, let's say, on the 1st of March. Now every day take the printed or cut out picture in your hands and imagine yourself on it. What are you doing, what sounds do you hear, what smells do you sense, and what light do you see? Touch the refrigerator, the furniture, the curtains. Focus on your certain actions in this apartment. Imagine yourself sitting on a white leather sofa with a glossy fashion magazine on your lap. There is a white saucer on a glass coffee table next to you, and you hold a white cup of hot coffee in your hand. You are not in a hurry, you are calmly enjoying a morning cup of fragrant beverage, flipping through a magazine, reading interesting articles. Have you imagined this? Capture this in your memory as a vivid picture. Return mentally to the pictures of your dream as often as possible; give them your attention, each time filling them with a light of love. Believe that by the 1st of March your dream will already have its manifestation.

You attract what you are focusing on. Quantum energy is always responsive to what we think. The sooner we realize it, the sooner we will be able to design our life and to create the reality that we dream about. Feel inspired and happy, as if you have it already! Fill the desired with emotions, without any restraints. Focus daily on what you want. Train your skills every day for 5 minutes at least. Add love to yourself and your dream.

I'm an ordinary girl; there are millions of people like me. But practicing the power of thought, I began to see more possibilities, and with them I became more inventive in my desires. Once I wished to act in a movie. I imagined myself in front of the cameras and clearly saw the film crew. One day I got a call and was asked to take a part in the shooting. It was a crowd scene, but in the foreground. I got exactly those emotions, I had been dreaming about. Arnold Schwarzenegger once said that every day he imagined himself being a successful actor and earning big money.

Almost every evening, when my daughter already sleeps, I hold my hands above her, imagining like energy of love is surrounding my princess. I imagine that we both are on the flower meadow, where the bright sun is shining I mentally pronounce: "All our wishes are coming true". Once my daughter said: "Mom, I know what you're dreaming. We both are on a field with lot of flowers and sunshine".

Love is a true reality, the embodiment of what you love. Love is the most powerful force, known to a human. Everything on the Earth and in the space is permeated by love. Love as a source, is responsible for the creation and manifestation of all in our physical world. Absolute, sincere love is a force that contributes to the materialization of everything we ask. It is very important to develop this understanding in order to begin to effectively attract your dreams. While you are praying, you experience the same emotions and vibrations. You ask not with a help of words, but by feelings and sensations.

Love every minute, making love the integral part of your life. This feeling will transfer you to another improved measurement, to the place, where you are destined to be from your birth. Love everything around you: the home, the colleagues, the trees, the sun, the rain, your neighbours, your car, your phone, your friends, your job, the colours, the flowers, the smells, the sounds. Make love your habitual state of your soul, and you will notice a wonderful transformation of your mind, perceptions and external manifestations. With a feeling of love in your heart you will begin to emit the strong vibrations of light, as well as inner power and harmony that will attract the right people to you and help you to create your own miracles.

Be patient with yourself and restful in the development of the inner love. Stay calm and meditate more often, arousing the feeling of love in yourself, when you go to bed, wake up, make breakfast, wash the dishes, go to work, check the homework of your child or go shopping. With each experiment of love you will move to the next level, attaching and increasing your inner and natural power. Pure heart contributes to the further development of your skill to manifest the dreams at the physical level as well as to the inner spirituality and harmony. The law of attraction works smoothly, if the vibrations of love come from a pure heart.

I'm not saying that you should strive for the perfection in your actions or thoughts and for the one hundred per cent positive perception of the world. Our usual behaviour and reactions in everyday life or at work quite often "pollute" our aspirations and the desire to be in state of love all the time. We begin to feel ourselves depressed or tired. I call you to the awareness, the vigilance of your thoughts and sensations. Having trained and developed the power of love in yourself, you will be able to influence any situation and completely forget about bureaucracy, lack of respect, lack of confidence, laziness, tiredness or what it means to be in a hurry.

In the book "The Messenger" Klaus Joehle proposes another view on reality. I like the story, where a man after filling himself with love suddenly realizes that in a shop queue people literally begin to stick to him. I can easily confirm that all this is absolutely true: when you are filled with love, you suddenly notice some lively interest in yourself, the communication becomes more active, and through this you notice your personal growth. You easily find the common language with people, they start to reach out for you, discussing some interesting topics, you realize, how beautifully you express your thoughts, and being once shy you suddenly have turned into a sociable and interesting person.

You should feel warmth and love radiating from your wishes. What you really want will certainly come to you, and love will fill the desired with the great power of attraction. Fill your dreams with the light of sincere and pure love, wrap up everything around with this feeling. It should be the love, which you feel to your child. You have these reserves! After all if you can love your children with this sincere love, then there will be the resources for such love for everything else, there is actually just One Source. And it is inexhaustible. Send love, until your desire is in the resonance with the energy of love by its vibrations. Desires begin to be manifested in the physical world, when they are on the same frequency with love, and in this case, you are creator, merged with the Source. Applying the absolute love, you attract to yourself more events, people, and situations, which you will definitely like.

Using the method of Jose Silva, I have learned to come out on the Alpha level with a help of which I have managed to attract a new job for my husband. He had already lost it a month ago, but unexpectedly he was offered this position once again. This was a real miracle and a wonderful change in the current situation. Alpha is a level, where the brain waves slow down to half of their frequency in a state of wakefulness. During a week each evening with slightly opened eyes I counted backward slowly from 100 to 1, thereby, achieving complete relaxation. And only then, in the altered consciousness, having reached the alpha level, I approached the owner of that company and surrounded him with light of love, being happy about the new job of my husband. Using this technique, I learned to identify the sensation, which clearly informs me that desired will soon come true; it already has its manifestation in the present.

Visualization in the present is the key to the effective materialization. In order to attract a big dream in the present, you need a proper behaviour and actions.

Do you want to have a better relationship? Then love all people unconditionally and look for those qualities in them, which would make you love and respect them even more.

Want to become rich? Look for those things, which will help you to feel rich, love money, imagine yourself wealthy and behave accordingly. Like everything you spend money on or invest. Like the process of investing money, whether you are paying the bills or buying food. Feel yourself rich, at any cost! Exactly feeling of accessibility, your inner state, will take you to the level of prosperity. These feelings will soon become natural for you, since you, like a magnet, will attract what you think into your world.

Want to be slim? Love your body, search for the ways to make it light and healthy!

Do you want your skin to be elastic, to keep it young and beautiful? You can do it using an auto-suggestion: shower strengthens the skin, cleans and heals it, and dancing makes your body look younger.

I buy my favourite cream and mentally give it an intention: it is the most effective, the best anti-aging face cream, which gives my skin the strength and shine. Sometimes I imagine myself in the old age, and I picture my future self as a beautiful tanned young-looking (!) lady with a gorgeous white hair, wearing a white trouser suit, sitting on a yacht in the sea. The breeze nicely caresses my face, which is glowing with happiness. Do you think, it is possible to be afraid of an old age after such an image or would I become sick and poor?

Cultivate balance and confidence, respect and love to yourself, develop your abilities through your faith to them. Your self-esteem is directly responsible both for the current situation and for the events that await you in the future. Your vision of future is limited only by what you think about yourself or something you can create.

Inspiration, action and choices

We have approached an issue of the necessary actions in the process of the dream realization. This part was absolutely incomprehensible for me some time ago, but now is my favourite in the process of the dream materialization. An impulse will help you to take some concrete steps. The fact that I love the sea, the sun, the heat and the sand, pushed me slightly to the idea of moving to the southern country. But I also wanted my family to feel comfortable and joyful beyond the limits of the usual place, so I have identified a clearer goal: we will live in the southern country, but we can always return and live for some period of time in the place we already got accustomed to, since we will be financially independent.

Practically each of us faces the problem that he does not know what he would like to do in this life. For a long time I also was beating around the bush. I was looking for the answer in the books about self-determination, searched for some clear guide, but every time I just rolled down to nowhere, realizing that everyone has his own way. However, after setting the goal to identify the vitals tasks, I have become more observant to myself and my sensations. I began to notice that I like to give pleasure to people through communication, and to some extent affect their lives. I also have been actively applying Reiki, if somebody requested a healing. And suddenly I found another way: the communication through a blog. But again, the more I laid out my thoughts on the pages, the more I needed some real communication. And that was my inspiration, my impulse, which led me to the organization of my own trainings. I have finally found my niche and began not to act, but to create. This definition, as it seems to me, better describes the nature of the actions that we accomplish, when we are inspired, - we create our world, by doing what we love. And I do not doubt that this is not the last stop, but a valuable experience on the path of my development.

The deliberate and detailed identification of priorities on the map of your life will help to find your purpose. Write down all your major goals, what you would like to achieve. Now think about something you like and write down these things. "Disconnect" from the world and enjoy the solitude, which is a precious time for the conversation with yourself, the acquisition of complete calmness and peace, the release of energy and creativity. Note everything that comes to your mind. You can use the example given here, but remember about the importance of independent work with subconsciousness.

To meet people
To bake cakes
To make jewelry
Laughter of children
To cook
Fashion design   To travel a lot   poetry   nature
music   House on sea coast
mosaic   Get marriage   flowers
sea   sun   mountains
To drive a car   To teach
To restore furniture   YOUR GOALS   To relax at summer cottage
To draw   photographing

Complete the map of your life with the answers to the following questions:

- What would you do having all the wealth and the right resources?

- What would you like to achieve in life in order not to regret afterwards, that you have not made this?

Answer questions fearlessly, do not limit yourself. The human is born twice: for the first time, when he comes into this world, and for the second time, when he realizes his own destiny.

Acting with inspiration becomes very important! Your impulse, your enthusiasm will prompt you to the right direction and to the necessary actions. Identify the primary tasks, make a list. To begin with let this be a list, compiled on the basis of your questions or intentions, for example:

- To find a purpose

- To become financially independent

- To find additional sources of income

- To find a reliable partner/sponsor

You need to define milestones, giving the universe clear instructions, which will carry out the list. For example, "to find additional sources of income" is not an indication for you to find them, take it as an order and believe that it will be executed. You should always remain open to the prompts and the new opportunities.

Realizing what you want, having converted your complaints into the intentions, clearly visualizing the final result in the present, you will attain the open contact with your subconscious mind and the responsive universe. Then take the appropriate actions which inspire you. These actions are intuitive. When you are inspired, the impulse draws you to carry them out, and you get pleasure from the realization that you successfully cooperate with the law of attraction through your actions. Limitations and obstacles disappear from your way.

Meditations, your inner balance, some visible and invisible assistants will help you to reach the harmony, necessary for the proper visualization. Remember, you are a magnet, magnet for the possibilities, the necessary resources, magnet for the realization of the right goals and actions.

Sometimes inspiration disappears, when we are busy with the daily routine or when we are looking for some answers. Make a break, grab a camera and go for a creative walk. The splendid views of our precious planet will fascinate you at least for two hours. You will return home washed mentally, all unresolved issues will go into the background or, better yet, will be already solved. Creative mood will last for a couple of days, or even more, and the muse, that has visited you after such close contact with nature, will materialize a paintbrush in your hand, and you will dive completely into the creative process.

Of course, children are one of the sources of inspiration. Games, walks with them, their enthusiasm will also give you a lot of exciting creative impulses. Feel free to proceed with drawing, writing a book, planning your business. Watch yourself: what else gives you inspiration? Communication with a pet, maybe going to a theatre or museum? Invest into your emotions and impressions, which awake a talent in you, entice you to the actions. Your deeds by inspiration will be filled with extra energy, and the result of your work will definitely surprise you.

Another important factor is your choice. Creating your reality, each time ask yourself: "Will it move me to my goal or not?" or "Will it help me to improve my life or not?" If the tax service has come to inspect your accounts department, for me there is only one choice. I would not argue with the officer, but would direct our conversation in a favourable direction. I would not be worried about our meeting's result, but I would send love to this event, to myself and to all participants. So that the energy of love and light would influence the quality of the event, and all the personnel would be impressed by my appearance as well as the state of my bookkeeping. And again this is my choice, how I would behave.

If you suddenly have found that the milk had expired, do not frighten yourself by the thoughts about unpleasant consequences, send love and quietly say to yourself: "everything is for the benefit". And yes, the milk will not be spoiled for you.

If you were in a hurry and did not listen to your child, but started worrying about this later, stop your inner dialogue, think that next time you will make a choice in favour of a happy relationship with the child.

Having seriously argued with the boss, do not worry, remind yourself that everything is for the benefit and next time tune into constructive conversation with him.

In any circumstances remember to ask yourself, will it lead you to the desired goal or not, taking, thus the responsibility for the movement in the right direction. But no matter what choice you will make, what will be the outcome of the meeting, or how you will behave, do not reproach yourself. "Everything is for the benefit" – this is the key to your improved reality.

A man lives the valuable life, when he has a purpose. What will bring you closer to its manifestation:

√   Sitting on a sofa or walking?

√   Painting classes or TV watching?

√   Another loan or starting saving?

√   To fry the meat or to prepare it in the oven?

√   To go to the party or to sale of the old things at the auction?

√   To give up some undertaking or to find a new solution?

If you are obsessed by the victory over your laziness, passivity, then with all responsibility make the most profitable choice for you. Make a plan of your actions. If you decided to write a book, devote at least two hours every day to this. Think, in just a few months you can have your first book. Do not worry, if at first you make little progress, the work on mistakes is also a valuable experience. The main thing is that you have defined the tasks and you carry them out, patiently, with giant strides moving towards the goal. The theme of the book will come to you as soon as you ask for it. Inspiration will guide your thoughts in the right direction.

If you are a specialist in your area, and you are always asked for advices, try yourself as a consultant, a coach, a trainer. Find your niche, which is directly connected with your habits and interests. You can create successful business using this. Make a list of the seminars or courses that you could organize in order to clearly understand the scope of your activities and to have an idea, what to offer the customer. Organize your first trial seminar in the close circle of your friends, but remember that in the end of the session the listeners should want to continue with your studies.

Maybe you love roses? Find the suppliers of seedlings, appliances for the breeding and the cultivation of roses. Create an Internet store or run a network of your roses distributors, organizing the "meetings of Roses" among the neighbours or companies. Unleash your imagination, and you certainly will succeed. You can create your own blog and write about cultivation and varieties of roses. After creating the website and optimizing it, you will attract visitors and advertisers. Usually well-promoted blogs in Finland, for example, bring about 50 000 € per year.

If you are enterprising person and see yourself in the information technologies, scrutinize the market, find some freelancers in the Internet and organize your own project.

Fond of photography? Check out all ways of earning on this craft. Study the art of photography and create your own channel on youtube.com, where you will demonstrate your skills, and teach the beginners. Let them be free at first, but with a time, when the ranking of your channel increases, you will be able to earn on the advertisement. Think about the field you like, you can take pictures of industrial buildings or butterflies, or maybe you will show whole stories in your photos. Grow in your direction, getting more and more inspired by the new discoveries.

Maybe, you have a story, which you believe will be interesting or useful for others? Get in touch with the publishers of the magazines, and your story, published there will probably increase the rating of the periodical, and to you will begin to get orders for the new articles.

Approach to the choice of your occupations responsibly, enjoy each new step. Celebrate each new achievement of the goal and thank yourself for that.

Your assistants

I wish that everything that you ever do or think would help you. Would help you to realize your dreams, to master the visualization techniques and attract the right things or events. I'm sending you love so that your hearts become open, and you feel the freedom for actions and for your reality. Let everything around you become impregnated with love, everything you look at or touch. Let all your thoughts be filled with love, they will become bright, and your presence and touch will become magic.

Your universe is your imagination, while your imagination is your universe! Trust the universe, trust yourself.

Take all the hints with an open heart, live colourful life right now. Look around you, you will see healthy beautiful trees, full of life.

They are miracles that Mother Earth has given to us. See how many visible and invisible energies or assistants are surrounding us and waiting for our attention.

I will give a few more practices and examples of their use, which will help you to gain a playful and happy state of permission or permissibility. You will learn to understand the language of the universe and to create the necessary conditions for the manifestation of your desires, you will learn to program your life.

The easier you take the work of the power of thought, the more natural you will apply it. And your new skills will completely change your mind, habits, and your reality in a good way.

Games with imagination

I remember being a teenager, I found myself in a bad company, and suddenly noticed that my worries went away, when I imagined a healthy green forest. This picture carried me away and at the same time drove out the disturbing thoughts. Apparently, then I was already unconsciously using the power of thought, and was taken away from the dubious company. My life became exciting and interesting.

When I decided to enter the university, everyone told me that it was impossible, that only one person from my town had managed to do that. This "impossibility" teased me and pushed me to try, at any cost. Keeping in mind my green forest, I began to imagine more and more often an efflorescent apple tree. Once I even had a dream about it. I think, the dream was a sign for me, and I was the only one from my town that year, who has passed the entrance exams. It was a strange set of circumstances, at that time I, apparently, had no purpose to study there (only to enter), and my parents wanted me to receive a higher education in Finland. So I left the university in Russia and departed to the country of northern reindeers (apparently, my green forest has materialized even then). How grateful I am to my parents for this! It was easy for me to enter the university in Finland. The apple trees were blooming as well as strawberries flourishing.

Let yourself dip into your imagination. What in your consciousness is associated, for example, with abundance? I think the first thing that comes to your mind is money. Answer now honestly, do you truly feel the ease and joy, imagining a large number of banknotes, or they cause some negative emotions? I think we are accustomed to think that money is bad, and it is quite difficult to fill the heart or feelings with sincere love when we suddenly see such treasures in front of our eyes. Therefore, I suggest you to try out my technique. Imagine, for example, a big fabulous oak, which is hung with the huge plums, bunches of grapes, mango, kiwi, anything that comes to your mind. It can be even a rowan tree, all hung with the ripe, juicy, bright red and heavy clusters of berries. This is your association of your financial state. Now every time, when you will think about cash in your wallet or money on your bank account, just imagine this rowan, hung with bunches of berries. From this point on your financial state is a noble, healthy, fruitful tree. A seed has not only been planted and grown, but also flourishes!

Let your tree work on you in all the areas of your life. Let the rowan become your symbol of good luck and success, health and career growth. Even being in a traffic jam, think about your good luck symbol and the cars around you will disperse, and you will not be late to the important meeting.

In the relationship an imaginary bridge will make you closer, will open a new development and help the communication. Beautiful candles provide romantic atmosphere. Drawing hearts (it is easy to see the connection here, isn't it?) will attract love. Healthy green forest will bring health, and the sun, for example, will open a new way, whether a new job or new journey, or maybe, will develop some qualities of your character. If you are lost or looking for someone or something, imagine a moonlit path. In Reiki, for example, there is an initiation of Moonlight, its energy directs mentally to the lost object. You can find it or light up the way home to a person. With a help of imaginary moonlight you can get out of the woods if lost, or you can find yourself, your purpose.

Play with the imagination, associating concrete desire with a picture easy for perception, creating new world, bringing a new properties into the desired.

Imagination is the power, which forms our reality. Develop your imagination by inventing the new ways of using different objects: an umbrella shelters from the problems, an iron makes amends for a fight, TV remote control rewinds the events, or switches from the quarrel to the peace and so on.

Together with a child arrange a competition: who will come up with more new functions for a kettle, a hanger, a carpet or the mittens. It would be not only interesting for your baby, but also useful. He will begin to come up with ideas of applying with great enthusiasm. Maybe, this will develop his designer skills! Just imagine, your new leather gloves suddenly became a sort of pots for the flowers, symbolizing the development of the child. Of course, first it is better to discuss the rules of the game. But I would say that for the sake of such communication with a child, your gloves are a truly worthwhile investment!

When you think about the abundance, due to your imagination your fridge will always be full, as if a magic tablecloth provides you with plenty of food. The imaginary rocket will speed up your career growth.

Dialling number 8 on your phone, you will be connected with the universe, feel free to say your intention!

Tune your radio to the frequency of the wish fulfilment, financial stability, high income or health. Or you can tune mentally to the channel of prosperity, imagining an antenna on your head.

Dreaming about being self-confident, I imagined the sun inside of me, as if filling myself and others with light and joy.

Write here three areas of your life in the left column below, which you intend to change. And in the right column - the associations that will manifest your desires in reality. See example:

Intention	Association of the desired outcome:
I'm a valuable employee, I do, what I have always been dreaming about.	In any case the tree with the fruit will be enough. But here is the second option:
Situation:	Imagine the sun (you clarify and illuminate everything), a field of the flowers (your activity has blossomed), in the middle of the field there is a huge star (that's you and your success). Now replace your current situation by this picture and take your job from now as "a star in a flowery field, flooded with sunlight".
You've got a job, but for some reason, you are not allowed to perform your duties and have to do some secondary work.	

Be courageous in your associations and keep the sense of humour.

"Me-naming", renaming, gifts

Authors V. Gurangov and V. Dolokhov give quite good oxymoron (comical effect) techniques to influence the development of the situations: "me-naming", the gifts giving and renaming. Instead of grumbling at your husband: "You are watching TV all day again, the dishes are not washed, the comb is lying in the wrong place", say to yourself "I'm watching myself again, I am not washed, I am in the wrong me". Surely, being angry after that would not be so easy. Well, men are like that, you always have to ask them to do something: "Darling, wash the dishes, please". However, you know, this is an example of our habitual beliefs: all male are the same. As soon as you believe with all your heart, that "my husband is attentive and loving", it will come true! You will enjoy your clean home, peace, and your husband will bring you flowers, without any reason.

In the renaming technique it is necessary to find something funny or an eye-catching around you and to rename yourself into this. Once I came up to the building, where I've been working, it was a sunny summer day. A bee, flying briskly and knocking to the cars windows on the parking, caught my attention and cheered me up. It was doing that so funny, as if playing. I renamed myself out of curiosity: "I'm a bee, playing with the cars". I liked my new name, and I entered the building laughing. There was a vending machine with Coca-Cola just in front of the door, which caught my attention. On a small screen I saw a furiously blinking text: "Ask for more". Near that inscription there was a factory code, which I have then split into the two-digit numbers and put into the lottery. And believe or not, exactly those five numbers of seven in the ticket matched!

When I was putting the baby to bed, instead of a usual thought "I will have to read for two hours to him again", I began to imagine my new name looking at picture on a wall: "I'm three dolphins, jumping out of the water". The child feels everything: he calms down and falls asleep very quickly when his mom is in such mood. The same thing is with the homework. Approaching the child with the thoughts: "Again two hours of persuasion and exercises", you get back exactly what you have "ordered". With trust to him, with an attitude "he is clever child, he listens to everything, understands everything, and does his homework" - you will achieve great results. If your inner state is anxiety or hurry, then you will not truly tune in. Deep breath will let you relax, as well as renaming, and what I love the most, is filling yourself and everything around you with love. This will help you to calm down internally and gain the harmony.

If you go to the dentist, rename yourself into "the glasses of a doctor on his nose" and the dental treatment will not be painful, because glasses cannot feel pain. Take a look around, when you go to the important meeting. Pay attention to something attracting your eyes and not giving any internal discomfort and rename yourself into it: "I'm a painted house sparkling in the sun" or "I'm swirling leaves".

Quite many people are "loaded" by imagined gifts from me. When my child went to school, there were some conflicts between children. They were arguing, who was a friend of whom, and fighting for the position in a group. Together with the child we have come up with the gifts for those, who were trying to tease him somehow or to cut out from the groups. The gifts were magical elephants, dogs, turtles. Giving gifts has become a natural way to change any situation for the better. There was one child in the kindergarten who was biting everyone, pinching, beating and scratching. When my child came home with traces of nails on her cheek, you can imagine my reaction as a mom. Do you know what I did? Every day I mentally hugged that child overwhelmed with emotions, I sent her love, gave gifts. Our children become friends in a month, and any weird story never happened again to my child. Having heard the details of that story, being already a school girl, my daughter was sincerely astonished: "Aah, and I was wandering, why she suddenly ceased to offend me". You understand that now she is studying in great atmosphere and her class is very friendly.

If for some reason, the meeting was unsuccessful or conversation with someone left unpleasant sediment, I give gifts in my mind, and everything comes back to its places.

Letter

Alternatively, you can write a letter about your possible future. Make a diary and use my example below, if you'd like. I highly recommend you to do this. We are not accustomed to think over the details of our dreams, and a letter will captivate your mind and will make you closer to the materialization of your dreams and acceptance of something you really want. Feel free to dream big, to describe all the details. Re-read the letter with gratitude and love, adding new colours to it!

Letter to the realized dream

In our new, bright, clean villa is very cosy and comfortable. Light falls into the house through the large windows. Beautiful sun rays are reflected on the walls and the floor. I'm sitting on a large, soft, beige sofa. I'm drinking a cup of coffee (what a flavour!) looking at the beautiful view from the window. There is splendour of lakes and mountain peaks, covered with light haze, just beyond the pool. Everything is filled with tranquillity and calmness.

Countless varieties of roses bloom in the huge yard. Their fragrance gently impregnates the house and excites the mind. The birds are sitting on the cherry-trees full of berries and their twittering merges with the music from the radio.

All our relatives are very happy for us, they like to visit us, and we are always happy to see them. There is a large guest house nearby, very nice and comfortable, where our parents like to stay, they practically live there permanently.

We have the best neighbours in the world. They are kind, decent, and always ready to help if needed. We can visit each over, discuss the joys of life, sunbathe, swim, have fun in the evenings. Sometimes we go jogging together along our calm and safe neighbourhood.

I love sport cars. Being once just a dream, now the new Lamborghini has manifested in my reality and takes the best place in our garage. I love to drive it and admire spectacular views.

Our daughter is fluent in the local language, she has good friends, and our life here is interesting and exciting. The school is close to the house, in about 5 minute walk along the street. Roads and schools are safe here. In general, wherever you go, everything is peaceful and friendly.

We are very lucky with the school! A lot of attention is paid to the development of talents of the children, especially to their creativity, the ability to perform on stage. Children learn to be confident and to communicate in several languages. Multilingual children get a strong support. This school is the best school in the country, the graduates enter the best universities without any examinations. The teachers and parents, experiencing limitless happiness for their children, communicate with each other, thereby creating the most comfortable environment for the children.

I love to work out a little after running in my large and bright gym (sometimes together with my beloved husband or child), and to relax afterwards in a sauna, Turkish hammam or Jacuzzi and to listen to the relaxing music.

My husband has own workshop, and his creations are in great demand. I do photography, paintings and write books. I have my own exhibitions quite often, and I get the orders for the next several years. In general, there is the complete harmony and in all areas of our life. We *travel a lot to the different countries for pleasure, and we allow ourselves a complete rest. We are surrounded by great friends, with whom we feel easy and safely.*

Continue your letter, adding the details of the interior, the description of furniture, facade, doors, listing your cars, yachts, clothes. Write about everything that surrounds you, make a picture alive by adding some action or a certain situation.

I let myself describe the interesting history of my friend. For several years she didn't have enough courage to move to another city with the whole family. She was only considering the possible variants. But once her desire became an intention. Nevertheless, apparently she still had some doubts, because the countless interviews for a job in another city did not bring any results. After desperate knocking into the closed doors comes the need to stop and think over, what exactly we are looking for. With the open heart my friend was confided in the universe that she will get a chance, which will open the way to the dream job, and moreover, the company will provide an apartment for her and her family. All these years I was aware of my friend's plans, so I was very excited to see the flash-like and surprising course of events. Staying in harmony with herself and inspired by her own actions, my friend suddenly realized, that a long-standing friend, the owner of one company was likely to have the job she was looking for. Just one phone call has suddenly solved everything. Exactly that vacancy was available at that moment. The future boss, who appreciated the talent of my friend, gladly accepted to take my friend to that work. Moreover, the company has provided an apartment in a nice and quiet area for three months free of charge. And the culmination of all this for me was the fact that this free apartment was situated next to my house, only in three minutes walking. And all of this happened in the capital region of Finland!

I do not get tired of repeating, that these moments are just wonderful, when you are in a nice company recalling a picture, that was a dream not so long time ago, and is so beautifully realized today. You simply had it in your mind and satiated with those emotions, which you are experiencing now.

Use of destructive energy

If, however, there are situations, when we are overwhelmed with the feelings of indignation and injustice, or maybe resentment and anger, - such destructive energy can be used for the good. In other words, we can transform destructive energy into constructive. It is worthwhile to mention that the world, or events and people that we come across, in fact, are not negative or positive. We make our choice of taking them either as a benefit to ourselves or as a harm. We always have a right to choose. Benefit can be extracted from any experience. Turning the destructive energy to the constructive one is positive, or more precisely, useful transformation made by our choice.

In the modern world we have been used to the following paradox: if you have no experience of working on executive position, then you will not get such a job. I seriously believed in this, and therefore I could not move forward: working as a simple engineer, I couldn't make a step to a manager state. But a chance was given to me, and I had to go through the numerous tests to the position, I dreamed about. The current situation in my life at that time caused the storm of negative emotions in me: I was breathless from the incomprehension and the injustice done to me. Destructive energy overfilled me. Having realized that, I summoned all my anger and threw it towards the materialization of the desire to get that job. Such a course of events changed my nature: I was so confident, that made a very good impression on the psychologists, who were testing me. I got a perfect recommendation, and my only minus in the summary of psychologists was – "sometimes she is excessively demanding" (normally I have a very loyal approach to the people and to the life in general). The fact of the transformation of destructive energy into constructive, was evident: I got the desired position.

So, if the incidents of the negative nature happen, use the powerful energy of your indignation: direct these forces toward the materialization of your desires. Remember, of course, that the good thoughts will return to you as favourable circumstances.

After realizing the mechanism of the transformation of destructive energy into the favourable one and having learned to use them, you will be able to direct your anger towards painting, for example, giving it some passion. This painting will fascinate by its energy, filled with inspiration of such power. Do not reject strong feelings in order to have a complete understanding of the taste of life, but know how to use your emotions in order to achieve your goals. Anger, as electricity, encourages you to "scorching" actions and mobilizes you to make a truly breakthrough, both in your development and in the conscious materialization of desires. Anger motivates you to destroy obstacles. Do not miss that moment, - this powerful energy can work wonders. But this may happen only if you are looking forward, and do not analyse the situation, do not focus on the source of your own resentment, causing the destructive fire of anger inside yourself. Turn the poison into the nectar.

You will suddenly find one day that there are no feelings of greed, jealousy or rivalry in you anymore. These energies no longer have their manifestations in your reality. The forces of these energies will be transformed into the creation. And passion will have its natural manifestation.

Ho'oponopono

Dr. Joe Vitale and Dr. Ihaleakala Hew Len discover a wonderful Hawaiian practice "Ho'oponopono", which I use very successfully almost every day in variety of situations.

Facing the obstacles, bad news, negative events or illness, we need to understand our responsibility: everything happening in our world was created by ourselves. Everything, including the injustice which is a reflection of our own thoughts and intentions. The meaning of Ho'oponopono consists, first of all, of the relieving, purification of yourself. And through the negative zeroing we directly influence all levels of our environment: intimate, casual-personal, social-consultative and public.

Keep in mind these magic phrases, which can be used in any circumstances:

I'm Sorry

Please Forgive Me

Thank You

I Love You

With these words, sincerely felt, we are asking forgiveness from the universe, the Supreme Reason for the situation. We tune to the channel of love by thanking and sending love, and the course of events begins to change. Ho'oponopono, thus, does not let the manifestation of something negative come into your life, as well as it has beneficial effect on everything negative, which has appeared in your world. I regularly use this technique in any negative situation, suddenly manifested in my life, in order to clear my mind, to create a state of emptiness, to feel the pure and sincere love. The technique can also be used, when you go to a meeting, a presentation, an interview, or to a doctor.

Purified, our reality becomes different, necessary conditions come up, as well as the favourable circumstances. In such world people start treating you with understanding and respect. They become friendly and see you as a bright and positive person. They want to communicate with you, to offer you a job, to sign a contract with you, to order your products or get your consultation.

Related actions

"Oh, my sink has turned into Mount Dishmor again!", familiar phrase, isn't it? What do you feel, when you have to clean up again? Dismay, irritation? Combine any routine work with the sensation of the progress of your goals, and you will enjoy all the household chores. Make it your habit.

When you wash dishes, imagine that you clear the space for new opportunities, ideas or some tempting offers. Mentally attract money by washing a plate. Improve relationships by washing a table. The passion and love may be united with the liquidation of the debts.

In order to attract money through related actions, you must understand that the law of attraction is connected with your views on money. If you change your beliefs about the money, on the subconscious level you will allow additional incomes to enter your life. Changing subconscious thoughts by associating them with any positive, even routine actions, you intercept all the negative emotions, associated with the financial state. It is possible to change the subconscious mind by making regular efforts. You will get used to the other feelings towards money, which will help the universe to improve your well-being.

You get what you think, activating the vibration of your thoughts. Take a candy, and all queues will melt away. Go to the shower, and it will wash off all your doubts.

Once we having arrived with our friends to a southern island for the New Year celebration, we have faced an unexpected trouble. Our friends' child's temperature has risen to 39C. The mobilization of all forces has been made. We wrote "high temperature" on a piece of paper and threw it to the floor from the table. The temperature, of course, fell down. The child has recovered immediately and after a couple of hours we all were having fun in the pool. However, I remember quite well the inquiring looks of other people, when our friends were measuring that child's temperature with thermometer from time to time. But, believe me, there were no reasons for worries any more. We all had a wonderful two week vacation.

Going to work along the corridor, I combined this action with a sense of being on a way to the success, directing my thoughts into the creative rather than routine activities.

Creativity and music

The state of happiness, the inner peace can be achieved by doing things, you love. I always loved to paint, so what I am doing now is not a discovery for me, but there was some kind of a miracle. Once I simply dreamed to learn the techniques and methods of painting, but now I draw information from the subconsciousness. And the miracle is, how I came to it.

It is well known, that the left hemisphere of our brain is responsible for logic, analysis, motor activity, and the right - for the imaginative perception, intuition, emotions, creativity. To achieve balance in the brain activity after work that requires concentration, I advise you to do some creative work, whether it is painting, photography, handicrafts, communication with flowers or a child, or joint family activities. When you reach a balance in brain activity, you reach a balance at the emotional level. In the process of creation you also develop the left hemisphere, which is important in the practice of visualization, it opens more and more unlimited possibilities and talents in you.

Miracles happen... I have heard this so many times before, but have experienced this myself only recently, having taken a brush in my hand. I always wanted to learn to draw water. I searched for "the lessons of drawing" on the youtube.com and started to learn. After a couple of days, being armed with a bag of brushes and acrylic paints, very inspired, I started to prepare... you will not believe, a wall at my home. Actually there were two adjacent walls and I began to paint right on them. Being in love with the sea, I wanted to paint seascapes, to reflect my memories from the journeys, to attract the view from my dream house on the sea shore. Music, a glass of wine, and my imagination went in the right course. I should say: to achieve the desired colour of water, gleams in the waves, I needed time and patience. But from the first strokes I suddenly noticed my complete detachment from reality. Inspiration led the brush, subconscious mind has woken up and showed, what colours had to be used. No wonder they say that deep inside each of us is an artist.

I remembered the inspired opinion of my friend about the courses of hemispheric drawing, I completely trusted my possibilities and abilities. Soon there appeared a coast on the wall, a mountain, a cave, a little river, some palms. I learned to communicate with the subconsciousness. Sometimes, wondering, for example, how to draw a coastal wave or pearl sky, before the bedtime I imagined this picture in my mind. The image was blurry at first, and then, suddenly, the clear and sharp forms just popped up. The next day I clearly remembered that picture, and the hand itself took all necessary paints. The unique things began to occur: by training the work of right hemisphere and balancing it, thus, with the work of left, my thrust to the creativity, ability and productivity has increased significantly. I felt the wings, and finally have gained the inner harmony that very well affected my family relationships, my inner state of happiness, my ability to work and my state of mind. Working on what I liked, I suddenly began to receive more energy. Accustomed to that kind of communication with subconscious mind, I caught myself one day on a thought that I have started to solve some life issues in the same way: trusting that the answer will come itself or I will get the necessary sign.

When I began to write my book, my friend advised me to listen to the music or mantra during the work. I completely agree: music soothes and tunes to the contact with subconsciousness, it implies the energy of harmony into our creations. With the writing of the book it is the same thing as with the drawing: after getting to work, your images suddenly begin to take the distinct forms, and work begins to occur at the subconscious level. The result of the works done in the sense of harmony and "meditative" state of love and happiness can exceed all expectations. Such works will be impregnated with beneficial energy, bringing luck, success and happiness to people. Everything is the energy.

Listen to your favourite music at home, in the car, when you play sports, at work wearing headsets. Music inspires and starts the little motors of happiness in you. For some period of time I used the same disk driving in the car. Those tunes, literally, brought to me the success: I was tuned to the desired wave very quickly, and important meetings went always successfully. Thus, I had a very successful interview and made myself look good. I'd like to add, that if your meeting went not so well as you expected, do not despair: turn the music on and return yourself to the wave of happiness. Thus, you can influence the negative situations in the past and do not let them spread in this reality by our worries or prejudices.

Use some musical instrument or take a simple pencil. Strum a song or draw your inner state and emotions from the realization of your desire! You will emotionally insist on the materialization of your dreams, by tune to the resonance with the Source through your creativity.

Signs

There are signs everywhere, everything you see around, absolutely everything speaks about your state and shows, if are you going along the right way or not, and what you should do to get closer to the goal.

If you see a controller in the public transport, try to remember maybe you should take care of some papers, and do it. If you hear from your friends that they are doing well, know that this is a sign for you: your business is also getting better. If you dream about having a new burgundy Audi, and you start noticing it more often on the roads, then you should become aware that this car is right on the way to you. If you get an advertisement of courses and it attracted your attention, think, have you considered some training for yourself?

If your work desk is not in order, - put everything on its places, clean up, and your working matters will get normalized. A stove, as they say, must be always completely clean so that goodies, cooked on it, would never end.

Negative events are the signs too. To remove their impacts always use "Ho'oponopono" technique. Such signs indicate that we should clear ourselves to stop the chain of negative events.

Signs or hints can be asked from the universe (but not forget to remain open) in order to solve certain issues. For example, you see two different ways, one of them is more attractive. You can ask the universe to give you a sign, which way to choose. When I was invited for an interview in another city, where I dreamed to live, I said: "If I hear Madonna's song on the Russian radio, it will mean that the change of the job and moving are the right decisions". In Finland, the Russian radio never played any foreign artists, but I wished for a miracle. Either my heart thus prompted me or something hit my head. You will not believe, but two weeks later there was a song of Madonna on the radio, but performed by Russian singer Alexander Serov and I heard it almost every time I got into my car. I did not specify the song or the singer, I just needed Madonna. That is how the universe can joke! During this kind of transformation periods we can also meet quite strange people. One a day, when I got a new job contract, I met a strange guy with a huge mop of red hair, dressed up in the bright colours. Of course, I took it as a sign of transformation, and we happily moved. When I started my career growth at the new place, before my next interview I asked "Will they hire me or not?" Then I met my neighbour in the new office, which was unlikely, and it was a sign again, that I would get the job.

It is possible and sometimes necessary to ask for the signs. To the question "Are we destined to be together with..." you can think, for example, that if it is so, the universe will send you many roses or will give any other clear sign. The bouquets of roses, in this case, can be seen unexpectedly in a street, on a television, anywhere. Just stay attentive to your environment, to everything the universe sends you. Your communication with it will let you understand what is really going on, and will also direct towards the necessary actions.

Once I have got an extreme sign from the universe. Now it is funny to recall, but then this was just outrageous! Being in search of myself, I wondered: "What can I do in this life so that it will bring a joy to me and other people"? I requested some clear signs. I was looking for something in a cupboard and suddenly, a heavy shelf, that stood silently for half a year, not bothering anyone, fell on my toe. This crucial barrier broke my toe! But during the sick leave I had time to think over this sign. And all the signs just before that. I have never been exposed to injuries, so I was wondering, who or what was trying to slow me down during such a short period of time. I knew, that the paces of the main job sometimes made my brain boil, but "to slow down" did not seem possible to me. Twisting as a squirrel in a wheel, I could not to stop for a moment. With that barrier came the realization, the enlightenment, and the chain of events led me in two weeks to a classical massage course. What was more interesting, I went there together with my husband. From the first lessons we started practising the massage on each other. By the way, I strongly recommend such courses for the strengthening of your relationships, as an additional joint hobby. The endorphins, obtained in this practice, will inspire and bring you closer. I was never planning to make the massages my main activity, but I always respond with joy to the requests of my friends and each time "refuel" myself with a huge amount of energy, getting back a miraculous gratitude for the relaxation, purification and pleasure obtained through my massages.

Omens and horoscope

We make up omens ourselves, for the benefit of the matter. Of course, we no longer believe in the negative result. Black cat is a sign of great success. To hear Madonna is for the career growth. Left hand itches certainly for the money! A neighbour has visited you - a signing of a new contract. If an interview is scheduled for Friday 13th, you will be definitely hired. I think the meaning is clear, we play again with the imagination and attract as a magnet what we think.

Go beyond the scope of your beliefs, create your own patterns. If a mirror is broken, it means that a transformation into improved parallel reality is on its way, so urgently and bravely go for a new mirror!

I want you to understand on the examples of omens the main thing: once we are responsible for everything happening, then all, we think, works for us. You are the information source, but not someone who imposes his opinion. Only you can guarantee yourself the result, in which you believe, not someone else.

And now relax a little. Because here is a horoscope from Elena. For which year? You decide, it can be used for every year. Believe only in good predictions, once you are keen on the horoscopes. You can also make your personal horoscope based on my example, complement it or make the one for each day for yourself and your family members.

Capricorn ♑ Capricorn

At the beginning of the year the elation and the impulse to take some concrete actions will await for you. Your ideas will be realized already by the spring. Do not reject the invitations to visit various events. A new acquaintance will be turned to a strong and reliable cooperation. In June, a declaration of love will give you a push to the creativity. Purchase something from the children's store, birth of a child is destined for you. Having rested in summer, be prepared for the new financial sources in autumn. In November some unexpected large amount of money will fill your wallet. Healthy sleep is a healthy mind. Pay attention to your dreams, there is a hint in them. Moving to the new place is coming in December. The 7th of December is a happy day. A surprise trip will enrich you mentally and physically.

Aquarius ♒ Aquarius

Communication with your close ones and friends will decorate January and February. You are capable of the transformation and of the new way of life. Arrange unusual evening, invite some guests. The purpose of the meeting can be, for example, sharing your ideas, or testing yourself as a magician, or an artist, or a training coach. Playfully wait for the salary increase in spring, and there will be the purchasing of a real estate in the end of summer. Your wish will come true on the 3d of September. You will be admired by others, so use your power of love in the planned matters. Golden autumn will truly be golden for you. Make December warm and cosy in order to give your relationships more romance.

Pisces ♓ Pisces

Music has a profound effect on you. Inspire yourself in the mornings by the sounds of your favourite tunes. The winter months will delight you with their surprises and pleasant meetings. Your lucky numbers are 7 and 3. You will be given wings in the lovely March, the trip will warm you and through the emotions will accelerate the materialization of your desires. Pick up the flow of love and grace, especially in the spring and you will harvest the fruits of happiness and abundance the rest of the year. You are keen in creating, and all the forces of the universe will direct you to the publication of your own book. The happy people will surround you, gladdening you, supporting your state of soaring. The significant harvest starts in June! Health will respond with gratitude for your careful attention to it.   Visit your relatives in summer, and the autumn will bring some wonderful changes in all areas of your life with a help of its colours. There will be a large cash prize in December.

Aries ♈ Aries

A fire is raging in you. Your enthusiasm inspires people for their own achievements. Your talent as a leader will be appreciated. The luck is smiling to you during the whole year. A tempting offer waits for you in February, accept it. Your plans are ambitious, and you have every chance to implement them. Mark numbers from the date of your birth in a lottery. You will complete everything, you have started, by the power of love. Wait for recognition, which will inspire you to a new exciting project. There will be new friends in

August, take their words as a sign and begin to act in September. Plan a vacation for November-December to bring you into a state of balance. Continue to inspire the others with your energy.

♉ Taurus   Taurus

You're standing solidly on your feet. Your inner state will be reflected in the real world in the materialization of a house or enterprise foundation. Your inner garden is paved with the new ideas. All ideas are destined to grow, you only need to send love to them for a good harvest. All year you will enjoy the fruits of your thoughts, do not forget to thank for that. Sudden sources of income will appear, so you should be attentive to the signs. The support of your family will give you confidences and activity. Spend more time with the people close to you: joint entertainment and leisure will direct your thoughts. Your persistence will lead to the goal at the beginning of summer. There are big savings in the autumn and the beginning of December. Probably there will be the acquisition of real estate, a store or a restaurant at the end of the year.

♊ Gemini   Gemini

Your eyes are sparkling. The state of love inside you lights up everything around, attracting new interesting acquaintances. People want to be a part of your life. Signs will tell you, whom to choose. If you have already found your soul mate, then a new milestone full of love and understanding will decorate your life together. February-March will be a life-changing months, in a good sense. Enjoy your work. The responsibility and love for your occupation will lift you higher. Join the courses in accounting and business, you have a gift of a leader. You will be appreciated as a professional consultant. Perhaps, this is your destiny? The summer months will be bright so you will remember them for a long time. Emotional, favourable mood of summer will affect the autumn period. Money bonuses will follow you throughout the year. It will be possible to travel again in December, you will save enough money for this.

Cancer   Cancer

This year, no matter where the cancer has crawled, forward or back, is a time for a pleasant surprise. The unexpected encounters, gifts, recognition, successes and achievements of people close to you will fill this year. Watch the signs, - you have a gift of healing both others and yourself. By the hands and the power of love you are able to influence the affairs of other people and to correct the situation. You have an endless energy flow, that's why it is always easy with you. The communication with you beneficially affects people and their lives. Pleasant journeys from May till October will give an emotional lift to you, bringing a lot of joy. The financial side will take a new understanding at the beginning of autumn, and through the gratitude not only you will be enriched by October, but also your loved ones. The numbers 16 and 7 will bring you good luck. The year will go in love, and some daily walks as well as your admiration of nature will rejuvenate your body, satiating it with good health.

Leo ♌ Leo

Your attractiveness will increase the interest of the opposite sex to you. Self-realization will begin from mid-January, your idea will find the necessary sources to be implemented. New strong feelings, unexpected gift of fate awaits you in the middle of the year. Be ready for the greater changes in your life. By the end of the year you will completely change understanding of permissibility in connection with the significant accomplishments throughout the year. Paying attention to proper nourishment and to the exercises, you will confidently step into a new stage and attract the reliable partners, with whom you will spend December in a well-deserved pleasant leisure. Health will be at the height and what about love, - you will completely trust the fate, and will be absolutely right! Drawing the "eights" will open the right way in any situation and create the necessary course of events.

Virgo ♍ Virgo

Virgins love to live according to the plan, everything is in order: at work, at home, in the relationship, in the materialization of the goals. Your indisputable help in business is your concentration and the skill to turn "nothing" into the tool of promoting your ideas. There is a significant increase of your ever-growing incomes in January. Reputation in business awaits for you, hence your popularity as a valuable expert in your field. In March your project will be realized, and the fee will exceed all expectations. The happy family and the support of your close ones will take you to a new level both in physical and spiritual plan. Contemplate the new colours of your life. The power of gratitude will bring a lot of necessary and useful sources into your life and your loved ones. You are incredibly lucky throughout the year. Health and love, as always, are at the height. Your lucky numbers are 20 and 9.

♎
Libra   Libra

Your scales this year will become your magnets. Everything you put on one bowl or another will be attracted in abundance to your life. You will feel new crucial breaths at the beginning of the year, which will give you energy and strength to realize all your dreams. Love, understanding of close ones, admiration of people will lead you to a new emotional level, where you will be able to manage your reality just by one thought. New hobbies become available, and the recognition of you and your work will bring you unknown income. You will find yourself in creativity, and the necessary resources will find you. Drink plenty of water every day so that your creative channels were enriched by your inexhaustible talent. Trips will give you new ideas. The acquisition of the real estate in August will create all conditions for your development. Your lucky numbers are 10 and 21.

♏
Scorpio   Scorpio

Move forward for the Glory – that's the motto of this year. Absolutely everything, whatever you will undertake, will bring success to you. Stage performances will make you more beautiful, more confident. The development of your abilities will occur with each new whiff, and there will be enough understandable and accessible possibilities to express your love for the life through your interests and talent during the year. You will be definitely appreciated and welcomed at any encounter. Your life is full of interesting events. Your life, which is your passion, will take you to the road and direct to the most favourable way. You will enjoy the flowers and gifts all year around. True friends will bring a lot of joy, the rest will be available when you want. 11 is your lucky number.

Sagittarius   Sagittarius

Your intuition will never let you down. Write all your ideas and fearlessly bring them to your life. Plan out everything and you will have time to it! Your confidence in people will exceed all expectations. Exactly your love will make your environment loyal to you, will create all conditions for the mutual understanding, support, happy relationship. In January a trip to the warmer climes will warm your mind and provide you with courage for new undertakings, bringing stable and good income. Your intuition will prompt you to the necessary steps, as soon as you will get inspired for the changes in your life. With enormous pleasure and calm confidence you will reach the goal by the beginning of summer, and you will start gathering in the harvest in the end of July. Autumn journeys will bring a lot of fun, you will be lighted up and at the end of the year you will have an action plan for the next year. The numbers 12 and 7 will open a new door.

The Moon, the Sun, the Light

If you have not read a novel "Brida" by Brazilian author Paulo Coelho, I recommend you to plunge into this world, where starts the communication with the soul. Having a solar spirit, I nevertheless tend to think that I am the Moon. It always fascinates me, attracts my eyes.

It has been observed long time ago that our ideas come to life during the growing moon, and the phases of waning moon let us clean the space for the new achievements, to grow new ideas. The Moon directly affects our emotions and sleep. If you want to start a new project, to buy something, to start a healthy diet, the growing phases of the moon (phases of your growth) will serve as a reliable foundation, granting all conditions for the successful visualization. Full moon is a time of power, the time of cleaning. This is the time, when the obstacles are overcome, and we are able to give up the bad habits or negative thoughts.

Write down all your intentions during the growing moon, select the most important and clearly repeat them three times, for example:

"I ask the universe to create harmony in my family!"

"I ask the universe to send me a large amount of money in cash!"

"I ask the universe to send me health/healthy heart!"

The water is controlled by the Moon. It is known, that the human body consists mostly of water. Hence the logical conclusion:

the lunar gravity, causing powerful tidal phenomena, affects also a human body. Many people notice that in the period of growing Moon, at the full Moon, they feel a surge of energy, and any obstetrician will tell you that during this period more babies are born. According to numerous studies, during a complete cycle the Moon brings different energies. Each of eight cycles facilitates the process of creation and manifestation. Eight phases are lasting for about 28 days in total. During the new moon, when it's almost not visible in the sky, energy of the realization and beginning dominates. Energy of the Crescent give strength, ensure the manifestation of the right resources needed to advance the goal. First quarter of the Moon takes up the fulfilment of a planned task. Energy of the Moon, approaching full moon phase, helps us to clearly define our goals, to draw a conclusion, to listen to the opinions and to make changes to the plan of our actions. In the light of the full moon either a manifestation of a wish in our reality, or significant progress towards our goals occurs. We can see where we are in the process of the realization of our desires. An evaluation of results, comprehension, and the right information come in the phase of the scattering moon. At this time share with others everything you have learned, since large information flow is going through you. At this time you clearly understand, what to do next. In the last quarter of the moon we are in the phase of the successful completion of the actions, the clarification of the actions launched in the first quarter. There is revaluation, we are able to identify the following necessary steps to achieve goal. During the last phase, the phase of the balsamic Moon we summarize all and discharge, without any attachment to the outcome. We do not begin new projects during this period. This is a good time for being alone, meditation and relaxation. We are clearing ourselves and preparing for the next new moon.

Observing the changes of the moon, I distinctly see its impact on my life, both in the nature of the events and on my emotional level. I do not argue, perhaps, the Moon affects me like this because of my thoughts about its impact. But, at the same time, if there is an active stage in my life, I would even say, the stage of aggressive actions, I do not need look at the Moon calendar. I know precisely that the Moon is in some growing phase. The Moon helped me to understand better the frequency of events or my attitude towards them. Now I do not wonder why some business is not moving forward in a certain period of time or why I do not have enough excitement. I deliberately use this period for not less useful activities: re-thinking, analysis or corrections. The reasonable use of a waning moon's period helps to promote all the pursuits more productively. This is the period of creative leisure, I would say, the preparation for the new impulses and actions. Having understood this period, we use it more efficiently. We improve our affairs with necessary attention, without any struggle to promote them at any cost.

Great!

In the Finnish newspaper I once have read a story, where the man who had won a million euros, says in the interview: "That day I joked and told the neighbours that they should come to celebrate my winning in the lottery in the evening!" A person on a certain emotional level is really able to attract into his reality something great with a help of one sentence or thought. I associate the feeling of that most emotional state with the word "Great!"

Do not be afraid to dream big. Feel the energy of joy and you fill your dream with it.

Great, I live in Switzerland!

Great, I have new Lamborghini!

Instead of thinking "What if it does not come to me?", "I want my own hotel, but I do not know where to get the money", invent the most unprecedented ways to achieve your goals, play with your imagination, coming up with more and more opportunities.

Great, the city administration has given me a land for my store free of charge! Great, I've got my dream job! Great, the washing machine works fine again! Great, we are friends with my boss! Great, I got a hotel in Czech Republic as a present!

By their nature, the high-sounding words have strong vibrations themselves, since they are filled with emotions initially. Their use helps to fill our intention with the missing emotional attention or impression; therefore the use of the big words will be only for the benefit.

Great, you will obtain success in all your plans!

Mudras

You can easily find the mudras in the internet. They will help you, for example, to improve health and immunity, to fulfil the desires, to make an eligible investment or to pay off the debts, to attract wealth, buyers, success, to gain confidence, to improve your memory, to overcome fears, to strengthen the heart muscles and so on. The mudras create specific energy configurations, setting an impulse to the movement and opening the way. In our case, let's look at Kubera Mudra, which is intended to fulfil the desires. It gives confidence in achieving the goal or wish fulfilment. Kubera mudra is dedicated to the God of wealth. You get peace of mind, imperturbability and confidence. Mudra also leads to the mental peace and the treatment of physical diseases.

Perform 3 times a day during 15 minutes, with each hand:

Join together the tip of your thumb, index finger and middle finger. The other two fingers need to be bend so that they rest in the middle of your hand. Kubera Mudra is practiced making a deep breath while inhaling, as if you want to perceive the scent of a flower.

Specify your intention clearly, asking your heart first, whether it will bring good or not. Then, while join three fingers, and, slightly pressing them, three times loudly say your desire. Feel the flow of energy.

My child likes "The head of Dragon" mudra (we call it "whelp"). If she has caught a cold, we immediately start folding up "whelp" with our fingers. The mudra is performed as follows:

The middle finger clasps and presses the phalanx of the index finger. Do it on both hands. Then, join the hands together. The thumbs of both hands are put together by their sides. The other fingers are crossed.

During the practice it is important to be relaxed, the back should be straight and your feet not crossed. The appropriate affirmations and visualization will greatly support mudras. Mudras can be applied anywhere and anytime. The time of session depends on you, it must correspond to the time of your inner dive. The effect directly depends on the quality of the inner silence, but not on time. Breathing should be slow and rhythmic. If you are using mudras to calm, then slow down the exhalation. Strengthen the inhalation, when practicing mudras. They will bring cheerfulness and improving of physical and material state.

Sport, massages

As you know, sport should be an integral part of our life. Physical exercises lead a person to the euphoria, the state of bliss. Massages also contribute to the production of endorphins (happy hormones) in our body. They improve metabolism and blood circulation. Both sport and massage, and any positive experience, in general, raise the level of endorphins in the blood. Exactly the lack of this hormones leads to the depressed mood. Have you ever noticed that after physical exercises you do not really want to fill your stomach? This is explained by the fact that endorphins, received during the trainings, suppress the thirst of obtaining the same particles through the food.

Having decided to get into shape, I first of all have hung a photo of a woman with a beautiful figure on a prominent place and have clearly marked a goal for myself: to go in for sports regularly. Three weeks later I received good news by phone: I won 30 € for the membership in a fitness centre. I immediately signed the agreement with them. The endorphins obtained at the trainings were so sweet that I ran to the centre again and again to get some more.

Massage affects the psychological state of a person in the best way. The mind and body are inextricably linked. Affecting people physically, massage affects the mental state as well: the illnesses are cured, emotional well-being is improved. A person, who gets massage, begins to focus his or her attention on "here and now" rather than on the problems, thereby obtaining necessary elements for the inner balance. The oxytocin and endorphins are happy hormones, so useful in our case. They are ejected into the organism after the massage session. The regular massage will bring out from depression, will put the nervous system in order, rejuvenate, give cheerfulness, improve the immune system and make you less susceptible to the depressions. There will be no space left for any kind of problems.

Visit the nearest fitness centre, where you will be always met by the trainers, healthy in body and spirit. They will greet you with a smile and choose an optimal program for you. Health is the first and the main investment!

Arrange a holiday for yourself, visit a massage salon, - your spirits will rise, you will feel that you are ready to remove the mountains after such therapy of happiness. And everything you have imagined in such a state will start manifesting in your beautiful reality.

Water and the healthy nourishment

Water has unique and a kind of magic properties. Water grants life, purifies, cures the diseases, and gives strength. The most important thing is to simply love it. Water reacts and changes instantly under the influence of the thoughts. A Japanese researcher Masaru Emoto notes, that water is cleaned the most with a combination of two words: "Love" and "Gratitude". A prayer, pronounced to the water, has a strong impact on the structured state of this source of life. Water is an essential element of our vital activity, because our body is 70-90% water. The lack of water causes the blood thickening, clots, our brain and kidneys are not washed well. Organism dehydration leads to fatigue and apathy. It is recommended to drink glass of water 30 minutes before the meal. This is even one of the methods of weight loss.

I would like to mention the process of making of Miraculous Water from the author of Ho'oponopono technique, Dr. Ihaleakala Hew Len (teacher of Joe Vitale). In his interview doctor tells about the magic properties of Blue Solar Water, which cures, heals and helps to cleanse the body. You can not only drink it, but also use for cooking, cleaning, or watering the flowers.

Water should be poured into a bottle or a glass of blue colour and then placed in the sun, in the open air for 30-60 minutes to absorb solar energy. Your vessel will be charged once and forever. When you are upset about something, drink some of this water, and you will instantly feel better.

Blue water brings you together with your inner child, with God, with the Source. The more you drink it, the cleaner you become. Add a few drops (or even one drop) into the meal of your pet or aquarium. Clean and give energy to your shoes or jewellery having sprinkled them with water. Spray a bruise or wound.

At any age you can change your daily nourishment, reversing most of the diseases. Turn to the healthy nourishment gradually, with love for your body. Proper nutrition will not only help to create a perfect shape, but also to feel yourself energetic and active. Forget about salt, potatoes, as well as everything where there is yeast or white flour. I assure you, a meal without fries can be also very tasty, even kids love it!

Surprise your friends with a cold soup:

Slice a fresh cucumber, add 2 crushed garlic cloves, a bunch of parsley and dill, pour I pack of kefir. Mix everything. Serve in beautiful glass with a spoon. You can add a finely chopped fresh cabbage, it will be also very delicious! A lemon will completely replace the salt.

Red Salad:

Pour kefir over the tinned red beans, add crushed garlic, chopped red bell peppers and tomatoes. Kefir with garlic, by the way, completely replace the taste of mayonnaise, actually it is much tastier, and better for health.

The most delicious rice:

Boil the rice and cool it down a little. Grind two fresh carrots, crush two cloves of garlic and mix well. Yum, really!

Divine vegetables:

Cut bell peppers, tomatoes, eggplants, zucchini, mushrooms, onions. Add a juice of lemon, olive oil and a few crushed cloves of garlic. Mix all by your hands, place on a baking tray and into the oven for half an hour.

You will like to eat properly, moreover, it is not difficult at all. You will feel lightness pretty quickly. Healthy eating will affect not only your look and health, but also your state of mind. Invent your own recipes, begin your blog diary and share your successes, making also money on the advertising on your website.

Laughter

Laughter has a profound effect on our body. Laughter is the best and priceless medicine! Laughter makes it easy to completely clean the lungs from accumulated mucus. Laughter can be used dealing with stress and depression. According to recent studies of American researches, laughter helps to reduce high blood pressure and cholesterol while people are watching funny movies or TV shows. Laughter generates healthy physical changes in the body, strengthens immune system, increases energy, reduces pain and protects against the effects of stress.

Laughter is contagious, it sounds more infectious than cough or sneeze. When laughter is shared, it binds people together, increasing their sense of happiness and bringing them closer. Laughter and humour help you stay emotionally healthy. In the laughter you will find the necessary strength. Laughter is contagious, - your brain will be happy to join your fun, thus, sending necessary signals to the cells of your body. Scientists estimate that only five minutes of laughter replace forty minutes of good rest.

Laughter is a natural part of our life. Babies begin to smile during the first weeks of their life and to laugh loudly after a few months. A person can learn to laugh at any stage of his life. In the laughter therapy, for example, it is not necessary to experience a funny event. The same applies to the smile. There are quite popular clubs of laughter, where people gather simply to laugh without any reason. Laughing in such groups eventually ends with a contagious fun.

If a person is cheerful, if he looks at the things optimistically, the world around him will change.   Insert humour into conversations, join bravely the companies, where you hear laughter.

It doesn't matter to the body, if you laugh sincerely or you cause laughter artificially. Every day, laugh heartily and loudly for 15 minutes! The hormones of happiness caused by laughter will make happier not only you, but others as well. Do not be surprised, if your inner cackle at work suddenly materializes in the form of collective loud laughter, - that is the reflection of your inner state on the layers of your surroundings. Go through life laughing!

MATERIALIZING TOGETHER

Having learned to enjoy life here and now, you will begin to materialize your desires smartly. Appreciate your skills even after the small successful results. We did not start walking immediately after the birth. We did not immediately walk proficiently. While learning, getting experience, we establish ourselves through the new knowledge, mistakes and success. Improve yourself, there is no limit to your achievements. Do not fall back, do not give up, do not refuse your dream. Do not stop what you have started. Go till the end.

Think of the practice of materialization as a kind of exciting game, the game that will distract you from the everyday routine. Life itself can be a hobby, but we should live it, so let it be a precious gift for you, you can create your miracles in it, so treat it with the full responsibility and the respect.

Exciting changes are happening already, no wonder you have found this book, and it has found you. The mechanism of the harmonious interaction with the universe is running, the beneficent magnetism of the book is growing through your memories of happy moments, your positive emotions, your laughter, your attention and appreciation of your life and what you have. So now, you can bravely go for everything you have dreamed about.

NEW CAR

What you do think, do you deserve to drive a car of your dream?

I do not accidently take a car as the first example of the materialization. Everyone wants a car, but at the same it is not exactly everyday thing in our life. By attracting a dream car, it is possible to receive a proper training in the principles of the law of attraction and to gain an invaluable experience.

Being a teenager, without driving license, I imagined how I rushed on a highway, listening to the music and enjoying the feeling of lightness and freedom. Then I simply dreamed to get the licence, but after getting it I almost immediately sat at the wheel. I got a smiling, turquoise, carefully wrapped "Nissan Micra" with a bow as a birthday gift from my dear parents.

Since then the cars have been replaced, as you understand, by the power of thought. When my husband and I planned to buy a new car, casually (or not) on our way to the showroom we decided to drop in and admire a brand new SUV, so that in the future we would keep it in mind. A silver new car flaunted in the middle of a hall. We were impressed by the price, but not as much as by the car. Realizing, that "it was love from the first sight" despite the thoughts about future payments and loan, we have ordered the car in two days. We have been waiting for couple of months for this marvel from Japan, and after having driven it for a month, my husband suddenly said: "When did you look at our dream map last time?" I had forgotten that once I made the maps of desires based on Feng Shui for me and my husband. I could not find mine, but another one was already hidden by my caring darling in a glove box of our new SUV. When I looked at the map of desires and saw our new car of a silvery colour, I almost choked with emotions.

It is worthwhile to perceive our children as our teachers, they can remind us about natural frankness in obtaining the desired. And the sooner it happens, the better. Being not aware of this, they rather skilfully send their orders to the universe. By switching to their interests here and now, games, chatting with friends, they do not tie to the goals, but release their wishes. If they want a new toy, they imagine that they already have it. Mentally they imagine a new bunny (seen somewhere), how they embrace it, while getting asleep. Or a new bike. In their dreams they see how they ride it. To become a child in your intentions is like affording yourself to have the desired. Recall yourself as a child or take a look at your dream with your child's eyes. Do you think now, where the money will come from? If you did everything correctly, and the feelings from the childhood awoke in you, allow yourself to materialize an adult toy. I remind you, it doesn't matter for the universe if you want a tricycle or luxury "Lamborghini".

Let's start with the reprogramming of our submissions. Imagine a child who has been given an interesting task to order a car from the universe. Let the dream car become soft and fluffy toy, feel happiness, with which you would embrace this bunny. A car for the universe is the same as a bunny. Experience the complete internal freedom of your intention, regardless the price of your dream. Be brave and let yourself want more. Energy of Money always flows freely to the goal, when the goal is defined. Make an order, and it will come to you in time. For someone it may take a year or years, and someone may receive it immediately. Everything will depend on the degree of harmony, I would say.

Let's analyse how time periods work in the materialization. You already understood that a sincere desire, which emanates warmth and love, become materialized. The more we fill our dreams with love (for example, we hold a picture in front of the eyes and say "I love, I love, I love" with a feeling of gratitude), the more harmonious our common world with that desired is. Entering into unison with the desire, "having rehearsed" with it, we do the materialization accessible, having created the harmony for its manifestation by the vibrations of love and by our own feelings. We can measure the vibration balance only with a help of our feelings. In Oxymoron I like the concept of "purring". Your desire responds to you in your soul tenderly and kindly as a kitty. A Krishnaite who conducted an introductory class of his religion, while I was studying, told and taught me to feel the answers by the soul. I memorized that the soul is where the heart is, but on the right side. If the answer to my questions is "yes", including "mine - not mine?", then I feel warmth in the soul. To like the desires with your heart is an important part of the materialization and timing. The greater the love is, the grater are the connection and energy between you and desired, the faster is the timing of your orders. And, of course, you can fill the desired with love as much as you want, there can't be any harm from love.

Now, when we have trusted the universe, let's define the brand of the car, its condition and colour. Let's take, for example, new yellow Lamborghini. Do not forget to attract it with the benefit for all. In the Internet we find a desired image of the car and print it out, then we attach it to our map of desires, or put it into this book. I like when the image is always at hand, so that I could hold it whenever I want, to run my eyes through it and imagine that I have it already. Then, if it is possible, we go to the showroom, take a test drive and buy… a keychain for Lamborghini! But if there is no such dealership nearby or you cannot order a keychain or even a cap via internet, then it will be enough to print the images of everything that you can associate with Lamborghini. Here again everything depends on your perception: someone will need to write an intention "I have (or thanks for) new sunshiny Lamborghini" and to repeat it; others will need a colourful picture or any attribute for the materialization.

Now there is the most important part. Right before we begin imaging the desire, let's dip into the creative visualization. What would you do, if this car was already yours? Going outside you would certainly first of all glance at your brand new yellow Lamborghini (with pinch happiness: finally it is yours!). You would click the keys and admire its cast forms, for sure, you would wipe it by the finger to check that there is no dust. How would you name your new friend, maybe **Alice**? "Oh, how beautiful you are, Alice, you are my talisman now!"- You would think. You will become friends With Alice, I am sure, and on the roads you will have luck and complete safety, because your car will be filled with love. Then, I think, you would get into the car, put your hands on the wheel, with a smiling and happy face push the panel buttons, yell joyfully and hit the wheel with your palm, shouting "YES!" Do not be afraid, I cannot hear you, but even if I could, what difference does it make? What kind of music do you like? Turn it on quickly, and loudly!

Having written, read, imagined, we already materialize. All of this already has its manifestation: what we have thought already exists **here and now.** Feel the wind in the opened window of your new amazing car, feel the music, the smells, a felicity that you experience with your new victory in the materialization!

Throw back the importance, this is a game, this is fun! To all doubts and negative thoughts we say: "get out, I've already thought about you". Settle there, on the right side, near the heart, a feeling of confidence, that the wish is coming true, it has already been manifested. The universe will be glad that you trust it. Feel love and happiness, repeat to yourself that you are the Magnet, you always and easily materialize the dreams.

Your keychain for Lamborghini can rightfully take its place where all your keys are. You can put it on a prominent place and take every day as a usual and necessary thing. Keep checking the parking lot, because there already stands your dream car. Behave as if you already have it!

I already feel the presence of my dream car in my life. It has sunk deep into my soul, and I always think about it, especially, when I rush along the highway.

HOUSE OF THE DREAM

The attraction of something you really want begins from a clear understanding of your goals. Let me remind you that the negative is not appropriate in the use of the law of attraction. If the negative thinking predominates, we have a low level of consciousness and energy. Dream House is a serious desire, a large investment, which requires a lot of work from our consciousness. It is essential to start believing that it is completely allowed to have a luxury house. Therefore, optimism and faith are integral components in the process of the materialization of desires.

So, have you already found an image of your Dream House? Now let's ask for it according to the principles of the law of attraction. First, we have to decide, what we really want. The determination of the location of your home is important part of the process. Is this house located in the city, where you live now? Is it close to work? Or maybe it is your second house somewhere on the seashore or near the lake, situated on the coast or in the mountains? How does your house look like from the outside? How many rooms are there, what do they look like? Next, imagine yourself living in this house. Think how you sweetly stretch in your bed in the morning and see the breath-taking view of the mountains and the lake from your window. All these answers, which you will find in your head, are the creative visualization that makes favourable vibrations for the universe.

The more you focus your attention on the details, the more you attract what you want. Imagine of what your daily life consists of in your dream house. Be thankful for what you have in your mind. "Listen to" the smells, sounds, and watch your emotions in this house. Ask for your dream House every day. Thank for it. Visualize it as often as possible. Imagination is a preview of what is coming into your life.

Be creative in your visualization. With your second-half get into the habit to discuss the details of your house every night, but as if you have it in the present. Start with a description of the yard, how the house looks from the outside. What kind of neighbours you have. Imagine that you greet them, for example, in Italian. Go inside the house together, imagining how excitedly you are discussing the day's events. Your dear children greet you and happily share their successes at school. Stroll around your house, go to the terrace, breath in the freshness of nature around you. Thoroughly imprint everything in your memory so that an image would appear subsequently in front of your eyes, and the new details would be easier to visualise. Being fascinated by the conversations about your house you will create a favourable environment for the dreams' manifestation in your reality. You will influence the events at the speed of light! Take responsibility for the fulfilment of your dreams, having provided time for the daily visualization.

Accompanying affirmations:

- My mind is totally focused on the ownership of my Dream House

- I believe in my ability to attract my Dream House

- I see myself in my Dream House

Having moved to the capital of Finland and living in a rented apartment, we spent the whole year in the viewing trips of the real estate being sold. We were looking for the property every day, but did not come across a place that would fully satisfy us. I remember, only once I noticed a remarkable new and colourful district, built in the Danish style, and I said to myself: "It would be so great to live in this area!" Tired of all that home previews which have already become a routine, we began to entertain ourselves by dropping into the beautiful places. And one day we see an advertisement of selling on a nice house in the district, I liked so much. An apartment, as Finns call it, was in the "house in a row", with its own entrance, terrace and small patio. My husband and I liked everything in it except the price. Again we started looking for apartments found in the ads, but focusing now all our efforts only on this area. Nothing could be compared with that apartment in the "house in a row". Not hoping too much, we went to see, if any other previews were arranged there or it had been already sold. And what do you think? Precisely at that time there was a new home preview requested by other buyers. We have not caught our competitors, but a real-estate agent made us upset: "Just before you another family has left an offer, and most likely, they will win, but you can try your luck". The sum, proposed to the salesman, is not disclosed of course; so I had to use intuition and suggest a sum, which would help us to get that house. During two days I sent love to the seller, the agent, the house, the bank, the neighbours. Two days later I got a call from the agent: "You have won, since you have proposed 500 € more than your competitors".

When my friends have bought a luxury house with a swimming pool in the yard, I inquired a how they had attracted it. It turned out that they had chosen the area long ago. As they wanted to live there, they went for a walk to that district quiet often. When they saw that the most beautiful house was put on sale, they immediately ran to the bank, doubting, however, that they would be given such a large loan. To their surprise, the bank gave the green light, and their friend decided to buy their former house. And all this happened in just one week.

I wished, my wonderful parents were living next door to us. Every day, leaving home, I imagined that they were already living in the house across the street. Every time the image appeared more clearly and sharper in my head. And in half a year my parents have moved from the city, situated 600 km from us, to this house. It is clear, that now, having chosen the next country of stay, I distinctly imagine in my visualizations our home there and a place itself.

HEALTH

There are many disputes about the benefits and harm of the modern TV shows about health. First, they say that the exclusion of some products from the diet is required, and in a couple of weeks we suddenly hear in the same show that the body cannot function normally without the useful substances contained in these products. I listen only to my inner voice. Of course, I often wonder about the benefits of some food, but only I can guarantee its positive impact, I'm a creator of my own truth. There is no sense to focus your attention on the negative result, thus causing the vibrations of negative impact. Having persuasions on a subconscious level, that salt is harmful for the organism, we create the vibration of negative impact on our health. Believing that salt makes our body look younger, we will obtain exactly this. I, again, urge you to a healthy nutrition, but, having made a choice, never regret it and you do not blame yourself. Use an intention: "Everything is for the benefit". For many of us it is difficult to change beliefs, for example, about the harm of solarium, and, thus, to affect the negative vibrations of such persuasion. But the intention "Solarium removes toxins from my body" might give a course of a useful purification. However, lot of interesting things about our health and the proper nutrition can be learnt from the TV shows, but the debates on what is useful, in my opinion, are not really relevant: everyone has own truth. Nevertheless, do not abuse the bad habits. It will not be enough only to repeat in the mind that salt is healthy, your belief must come from the subconsciousness. Think more about what is really beneficial to your health. When you have a responsible approach to what is going on in your life, you will no longer want "to stuff" yourself with harmful substances.

I will not be afraid to reveal the theme of cancer, its causes and ways to recover.

Any disease can be caused by hypochondria and emotional state. Suggestive power of love acts in times stronger than any negative thought. With the energy of Love, Prayer, we are able to influence beneficially any situation, no matter at what stage it is at the moment.

There are all the chances to win over the cancer. This disease can be seen as a clear indication that it is necessary to change the worldview. And thereby there are great chances of recovery, if the patient makes every effort to recover and to rethink the values of life. The awaked love for life is a magic key, which will open the door to the recovery. Cancer is caused by old resentments, anger, pain, hostility, "inside worries" that eat up a person from within by their destructive energy. But it is worthwhile to thank for such an experience, to accept this as a sign and a chance to change. That is why there is a saying in the modern world: "Fall in love with your illness". Even if you were prescribed chemotherapy, do not doubt to go for this treatment. Imagine that the radiation is a cosmic curing ray that aggressively destroys cancerous cells during the therapy, fills you with energy of the divine light and with elements promoting the healing. Dispose yourself that your body will be fully recovered after the treatment.

Ho'oponopono, Reiki, Love, Prayer, joyful emotions, forgiveness and deliverance will help to come cleansed and to accelerate the recovery.

Ask and it will be given to you. Send Reiki or love to your apartment, to the bed, where you sleep, to everything that you eat or drink, to the visit to your doctor, his office, to the road to the doctor, to the tests, to everything that surrounds you. Send love to the disease and to each cell of your body, to all particles. Repeat, that your life is interesting and that you love and appreciate it. Thank your world for the fact that it is with you.

Traditional Chinese medicine says that the human body operates on the basis of the energy channels, the so-called meridians. All processes in the body are controlled by the energy flowing through these meridians. When a person experiences disease or any type of indisposition, the energy flow is blocked. In order to establish harmony these blocks must be removed.

Stress and negative emotions prevent the energy flow normally throughout the body. If the energy channels are blocked, the visualization of the transition to a healthy state becomes complicated. Our mind cannot focus on the manifestation of the desired result. It is actually to liberate the channels from the blocks, the visualization plays, again, a key role here. It is capable to direct subconsciousness towards the creation of the images, required for the purification of energo-informational shell.

One of the most common ways to restore vitality is to visualize a golden sphere that performs the function of the purifying the channels from the negative energy, which was gathered for the various reasons in the body.

Surround yourself or the disease with the imaginary golden sphere. Its energy will produce the cells necessary for the recovery and will help the healing process. Attention, don't forget about the doctors, but some actions accompanying the recovery will exert the beneficial effect.

The technique "Golden Sphere" can be used under any circumstances. Form a golden sphere around yourself and take up the process of healing. Fill the sphere with a golden light. Keep the image and begin the healing through "prana" breathing. You can express the intention to heal yourself. For me, it is enough to imagine the golden sphere in my throat, if it aches. You can also imagine someone of your close ones in the golden sphere, if they need such a help. This technique does not require any prolonged preparations, special skills, it is easy to use. The duration of this session will be suggested by your intuition.

Prana breathing will also cause the feelings of love and healing in the divine light. Imagine the golden light coming in through the crown of the head, when you inhale. Allow the energy to go through your whole body. Exhale after a few seconds and you will let the light go out through your heart. Slow breathing gradually. You can determine the duration of this practice by yourself. Prana breathing will also help to calm down and to focus as well as connect with your higher self and the source of your guides.

Another equally effective technique is, when a man in relaxed state of mind mentally enters the source of disease or the place, where the centre of the pain is. Looking around, you will notice not only the condition of this part of the body, but also the energy of imbalance, specific emotions associated with the pain. Recognize the pain and ask yourself what could cause the disease and what will help to free you from this pain.

Inspired by new events in my life, successful progress of my business, completely fascinated by the use of the power of thought, I, suddenly, felt a sharp and aching pain in my tooth. "What's going on?" I thought. "My internal and external worlds no longer contain anything negative!" A doctor recommended a treatment of the tooth root. I've become really upset (I'm afraid of this type of treatment), and decisively studied my thoughts. Tooth root, as I thought, is, most likely, a manifestation of something that is connected with my roots or relatives. I had to "ground"! Having plunged into the details of my life here and now, I gratefully looked at my relationships with the relatives and wished them love and prosperity. Mentally I entered the tooth root, and having filled it with the energy of joy and love, I asked it for forgiveness, thanked for the sign for me and made a declaration of love for it (Ho'oponopono technique). The pain continued for two days, but I kept repeating the words "I'm sorry, please forgive me, thank you, I love you". On the third day I decided to go for the treatment, but something was prompting that the treatment was not necessary... And so it happened. After the X-ray photography the doctor said: "Everything seems to be fine, no treatment is required" and my tooth stopped hurting the next day.

It is worth mentioning the story from the Russian TV show "The Battle of Extrasenses", where American Veet Manoi gives truly correct parting words, and a prediction for a girl suffering anorexia. I believe that there are extrasensory abilities, and everyone, if desired, can develop them. I think that these people have abilities, grafted or developed by using the power of the thought, and they use the appropriate methods and techniques, convenient and accurate for each of them. Some people believe that they receive the information from the subtle world, in fact, they materialize phantoms and communicate with them, getting truly accurate information. Others believe that they can heal people through the power of love, see the previous or future events in a state of an altered consciousness, and it really happens in their reality. Many people with such abilities can be true professionals, magicians in their work. However, the behaviour of the extrasenses, unfortunately, is not always ethical. After all, they say that it is impossible to predict the future, because it can always be changed at any moment, so it depends only on the means of our thinking. Hence a conclusion - an extrasense, possessing the gift of seeing the past, must direct the person's thoughts towards the improved transformation of situations as well as give the necessary recommendations: to forgive, to thank, to love. There is not spoiling, envy, diseases, and misfortunes in the future, until a person himself believes in them or creates them by his thinking. However, being under the influence of an experienced ekstrasens, people start to believe in the predictions, thereby embodying them into reality. In my opinion, this is incorrect motion from the part of people with extrasensory abilities. Veet Mano helped the girl to reveal the cause of the disease, which, as it turned out, came from the childhood, when girl was suffering from an inferiority complex due to the pressure of the circumstances. She wanted to be a boy, so she has blocked an energy channel in herself, having de-energized organs. Mano felt the cause of the disease, helped to remove the blocks and predicted that she will get well. Already during the session the girl said finely that she was hungry.

"What is happening to me?" - I asked quite may years ago my friend, "how can a conflict situation arise out of nowhere, or how can I suddenly have earache and fever, while I am actively practicing the power of thought?" She answered me directly and honestly:

"You are not grateful". I wish you to have friends like that, who can admit your mistakes, tell you about them so that you could figure out how to get out of a maze. My friend affected many areas of my life with just one sentence. When I went to the doctor with the sick ear, I was hoping that it would be some kind of magician, because I did not want to hear the banal "you have an inflammation". I needed a specialist practicing the power of thought. When an Iranian doctor examined me and said: "You are allergic, you do not want to hear something", I was ready to kiss him! He added also a remarkable phrase: "All diseases are caused by the allergies, all medications at the pharmacies are from the allergy". I was jubilant while walking home. That doctor was, probably, from some parallel reality, since for Finland it is an exceptional case for a doctor to point out aloud the patient's thinking. Well the cause of the disease was found: I was really ungrateful to those, whom I did not want to listen to. I was allergic to the circumstances. And all this happened because of my ingratitude. It was an invaluable lesson. Soon the relationship with those people, with whom I had had a painful conflict, reached a new level, full of mutual understanding, love and harmony.

When you communicate with own body, with your inner world, you will find the cause of the disease, you will reach harmony with your body, and it will become more easy to visualize it healthy. Your body just tells you that it is trying to do everything possible to adapt and to find a balance, so please help it. Remember about the purification from the negative thoughts, grievances. A person, who is in harmony with the world around him, will be full of strength and vital energy.

We are very good friends with our neighbours. It is nice to know that in spite of the fact that we live in a foreign country with its own culture, we nevertheless feel ourselves very comfortable with the people of another nationality. It means a lot: if we admire our neighbours, can be close friends with them, find a common language and be ourselves, Russians, this means that we are wonderful too. Our neighbours are our reflection.

I haven't seen one of my neighbours for a while, and when I accidentally met him, I was shocked: he was haggard, with hollow yellow eyes, barely able to walk. He reassured me, that he was already getting better. Soon the situation has repeated. And for the third time I started reflecting. There is something wrong in my life. Knowing that all the diseases, in some point, come from the stress, I re-examined the books of Louise L. Hay, Valery Sinelnikov and other authors, and have learned, that a liver disease can be provoked by a loss of energy, when a man desperately goes to the goal, forgetting about everything in the world, thereby harassing himself in this struggle. The accumulated bitterness from the disappointments on the way to the goal leads to the disharmony of the liver function. Rather than adapt to the situation, a man begins to experience anger and rage, but at the same time he attempts to suppress emotions, destroying thus himself from within. I realized that my neighbour has faced exactly this type of problem. I do not think there were such negative emotions, but I saw how busy he was, how he was trying to create the most comfortable environment for his family. At the same time I realized that, since this came to me as a sign, then correspondingly, in a certain degree, my energy flow was disrupted too. I was in a rush going towards the goal at a stunning pace, wanted to become financially independent. There was no disappointment or anger in me, but I with my own affairs I forgot about the life here and now. My family remained without my attention, I spent all the energy on the achieving of my goal. I mean sincere attention that is "present", and not fleeting. Grounding is necessary, when we "steep" in the business. Always remember about the life here and now, be sincerely grateful for what you have: for the happiness in the family, for the bird, tweeting at your window, for the health of your loved ones. Spend more time with your family, friends, go for a walk and communicate with the nature, and do not forget about the present.

When I recalled this wonderful rule, I immediately felt better. Having applied Ho'oponopono for myself and for the neighbour, I went to visit them. Do not think that treating others with the energy of love or Reiki takes away the energy from the person who gives it. It is not necessary to believe in the positive results during a Reiki sessions, but the desire of a patient to receive Reiki is an obligatory condition. Since I have met my neighbour in such condition that time, I knew that I could affect the situation. This is my world, something is not going right in it, and healing him, I would level off the structure of my energy. Yes, oddly enough, selfishness and altruism are merged into one in the law of attraction, but there was a sincere need to help our friends in my motives. I was simply aware, that doing good to others, I will also do good to myself.

Within a few month every other day I visited this lovely family, gave a Reiki session, worked on a neighbour's body and his emotions. I thanked them after each visit for the experience and the strength I gained. I felt like I rediscovered myself after each session. My strength increased, more and more I began to feel the invisible help from the other side as well as received the powerful energy from my neighbours' sincere gratitude. Believe me, I also had a lot for what I could thank them for. Ho'oponopono was also included into treatment as a compulsory element.

I cannot describe the happiness on a face of the neighbour's wife, when she told me about their next visit to the doctor. Sitting in the lobby of the hospital, she just mentally repeated non-stop: "Thank you, thank you, I love, I love". And here was the first good news! Firstly, they have finally met a good doctor, who lucidly explained what was going on and reassured that there was nothing to worry about. Secondly, the tests done, finally, got better, and the liver started to recover. This was the first victory! Before that there even arose a question of a liver transplantation.

The neighbour's wife has clearly marked the date of the full recovery - Christmas, the magical time. And right after Christmas the neighbour was again engaged in the business. I have been spiritually enriched, purified, and have balanced my world. Thanks to my wonderful neighbours.

We all have an ability to heal people. Do not be afraid of it, we should feel happy when we help people. The more we work on the world improving, the better and cleaner becomes our reality and we ourselves.

Again, all the techniques, I have presented here, should not be used as a complete self-treatment, but only as an additional help to the treatment prescribed by a doctor.

The eternal question: how to lose weight? It is actually easier than we think. We gain the excess pounds, when we are experiencing self-pity. Would you agree that when we believe that we do not have enough time, are in a stress and feel pity for ourselves, as a consequence, we get nervous, thus creating disharmony in the body. When we practice the principles of the law of attraction and expertly enter the state of emotional balance with the world around us, we affect our health directly, in this case the proper metabolism of our body. Thinking positively, without a fear or irritability, we create balance in the body … and begin to lose weight.

Obesity is a kind of protection, when a person is being asked for too much. The cause can be found in the childhood. Nevertheless, the identification of the disease and its cause are the first steps on the way to recovery. The disease is an abnormal flow of life, and when a person' changes his worldview, the disease steps back. Constantly repeat in your mind: "I'm loved and respected". Fresh air, exercises will enrich you not only physically, but also on the emotional level, you will become more resistant to the stress. In addition, by using the power of thought, you can also give your muscles a beautiful shape. You can lay on a sofa listening to the music and visualize, for example, the press swinging. The effect will be the same as in a gym, if you will do this regularly.

Healthy eating will stimulate you, and without doubt a deferential attitude to your body will be reflected on your well-being. Make it a habit to drink the elixir of youth and health every morning on an empty stomach. Put a tea spoon of honey in a glass of warm water, and if desired add a lemon and some ginger root.

If you eat the carrots every day, you thereby stimulate the growth of the healthy cells, strengthen the immune system and reduce cholesterol in the blood. Carrots contain a substance belonging to the family of endorphins, and endorphins, as you known, have a stimulant effect on the pleasure centre of our brain.

Drink two litres of water every day. It is worthwhile to replenish the water in the body, as you will immediately feel yourself better. Water also contributes to the recovery, because its properties can become magical. For example, "addressing" the water with the words "I love, I love, I love", we will improve the quality of water and fill it with the energy of love, thus giving it a favourably influencing properties. As you remember, drinking water, which contains the specific information, for example, the words of gratitude, a person can significantly change his state. The structure of water varies depending on its "impressions", and at the same time, filled with the positive thoughts, heals the body and soul. Fill the water with the energy of love while taking the shower, cooking, washing dishes, watering the flowers etc.

Our conscious choice will allow us to achieve the desired result.

RELATIONSHIP

We will not talk about relationship, but about interrelationship with the world around us. In fact, it is important to understand the harmonious interaction of the components in the environment where we live.

There are no good or bad people, we either create the character for them in our mind or attract them into our reality for some reason. Everyone has his own casual-personal, social-consultative and public spaces, everyone has his own experience and beliefs. Therefore, the disputes between people are meaningless. Everyone has his own truth, and everything happens in a person's world according his or her beliefs. Children grow, get their own environment and go out of the casual-personal space of their parents, many of whom begin to wonder why they had lost mutual understanding. In reality, the acceptance of such natural transition of children into the adulthood can lead to the recognition of your children as the independent personalities, which will serve the development of harmony in communication and mutual trust.

The main thing in the relationship is understanding and respect. Having internal balance, we attract to ourselves the right people with whom we feel comfortable. If we are always tired, then we will see boring and tired people around us. If we are inclined to complain, then the eternally complaining people will surround us. If we are interested in sports, then there will be athletes in our environment, who have the same spirit. If we are fascinated by the paintings on walls, then it is not surprising that we will see more and more creative people. Understanding these principles of the law of the universe and, following the simple rules, we will be able to live among the smiles of successful and good people.

If we have created everything that surrounds us by ourselves, then we and only we can change it. If we are offended, then would it be right to blame another person, if there is our own reflection in front of us? If we are responsible for everything that happens to us, would it be correct to blame our environment? And furthermore, it also makes no sense to blame ourselves. By using constructive, not destructive energy of the positive thoughts we can change our world for the better. If you have a small pension, you will be given an unexpected permanent income, the best and the most intelligent teachers will teach your children, you will meet only friendly sellers in the stores, and you will be the first to be given a place in public transport.

Smile to people, smile, even when no one sees you. Smile to solve the most important issue, smile while making phone calls, even when you hear only beeps yet. During the conversations as well as in your letter your smile will be "heard", and you will be responded accordingly.

Getting along with people should bring you pleasure. Think if there still is someone always complaining about his life in your environment, maybe you should change something in yourself or give up this kind of communication? Do you have a colleague or a friend who likes to shift the responsibility for his own problems on you, complaining to you constantly? Start from the small: tell such person that you've got some things to do, you are busy. Get out of this annoying conversation that doesn't carry anything positive. Paying attention to the problems, even if they are not yours, you attract these problems into your life. And this is not a refusal from sympathy, which is a quality of a nice person, but a help to "erase" the negative from your life and the life of that person, who complains. You will soon find out that people around you are happy. They will say to you: "It is so easy and comfortable with you, there is no need to discuss any problems", because you will attract such people, and the worldview of those having complained earlier, will be changed. But if a person does not give you anything back except the negative emotions, do not hesitate to give up this communication.

At some point, I suddenly became assailed by unpleasant and strange sensations. I honestly and fully acknowledged them, but it was not helping me. The whole point is that having a clear understanding that everyone is responsible for his life, I got a prejudice towards the people, who seemed to be ungrateful for what they have and created all sorts of troubles for themselves. And again my friend helped me to expand my mind: the fact that these people exist is already a kind of their mission, and they are already grateful for their earthly incarnation. Having different addictions or creating a mess in our peaceful existence, these people perform their functions, making someone stronger, directing us, carrying a reflection of our thoughts, sometimes fears, disappointments, prejudices. Therefore, meeting such people should be taken with gratitude. In the essence, they create a balance in our thinking. If we "fall out" from the harmonious existence, an imbalance of energies takes place, and the people that cause suddenly indignation in us by their behaviour or their way of life, provide an opportunity to review our own life. By their appearance or, even if they are close to us, by their actions and behaviour they contribute to the adjustment of our own life, and through us - of their own. And because of this it is worthwhile to be grateful to them. Do not blame them. Help them with your thoughts, which are material.

With my beloved husband we have a silent agreement: if some unpleasant situations occur at work, we can discuss the feelings at home, but it is prohibited to talk about details, to "grind the stones". Why should we pay attention to something we do not want to develop! It is possible to recognize the problem, but only in order to understand what has caused the manifestation of this situation in our life. "Now I am less irritable at work", - my spouse agrees, "and the atmosphere at work became more calm". When his boss has some kind of critical days and emotions begin to overfill him because of misunderstanding, I send love, success in the business to all the superiors of my husband, I mentally embrace them. I can only imagine a stunned boss, who is sitting surrounded with love and he does not understand, all these bright feelings come from. Naturally, all conflicts become solved by themselves.

Criticism is a powerful tool. Sometimes an underestimation of our abilities pushes us to the new achievements, therefore, as I always say, a person who does not hesitate to express his or her criticism in your face is a valuable friend. You begin to be driven by the passion in promoting your goals. You try to prove first of all to yourself that your idea is worthwhile. One of the auxiliary elements here is a state of "grounding", when analysing the criticism, you get down to the ground in order to once again consider thoroughly your decision or action. Criticism is our bread, but never let it stop you from moving forward. Again, we choose by ourselves, in what way we will use the critiques.

Be the one who brings happiness to others. Make it pleasant to be next to you. Answer the simple questions in the affirmative: you are excellently doing at work, there is harmony at your home, and you have always enough energy and time for everything. You will begin to believe in these statements and the favourable changes will come by themselves, new interesting people will appear in your life, and well-being will be guaranteed to your family.

If you have an executive position, treat your specialists with great care, respect and trust them. Noticing the professionalism of all the participants, having a confidence in the successful completion of all affairs, you will achieve the desired results. A detailed work plan will be a reliable support to you. After the completion of a project it is necessary to thank everyone for the excellent cooperation.

An attitude of others towards you can be controlled with the power of thought, you can even manipulate the opinions of others, - it is our own choice what really happens. We become what we think about ourselves. We are taken in the manner we imagine or we allow. We see what we expect to see.

LOVE AND FAMILY

Having filled and surrounded yourself with the magical power of love and gratitude, you will be amazed by the surprising changes. Your personal magnetism will attract the loving and sympathetic hearts to you. The universe likes to surprise: the wishes usually come true in the most unexpected and miraculous way.

If you want your second-half looks like a movie star, feel free to print the photos of him or her and put them into this book. Look at your future spouse every night and pay attention to your life together, visualizing your breakfasts, walks, something you will do together, your family traditions. Be prepared for the encounter with your destiny. Choose a place, where you will wait your soul mate, for example, in the woods, in a cafe, in a library, in a bank, in a theatre, on a bus stop or in your office. Believe that the meeting will necessarily happen. Prolonged waiting can cause discomfort and disappointment, but remember that being in harmony with yourself, without experiencing stress or negative emotions, you will accelerate the manifestation of the desire. Believe in it, but do not get attached too much to the goal. Release the situation and do not let the doubts disappoint you.

Let's say you have chosen to come across your second half in your favourite fitness centre. I think it will stimulate you to have the regular exercises in the gym, so the visualization will be not only pleasant but useful too. Since now you will train, carrying out simple tasks to attract your beloved one into your life. Imagine an encounter and your mutual attraction, dream about living together.

Add love, tenderness, passion to your images. Develop a state of anticipation both of the meeting and of your life together. Visualize that your each move in the gym approaches the moment of your acquaintance, adjusts to the wave of love and affection, faithfulness and prosperity, trust and mutual understanding. Think of your beautiful wedding and your cosy nest. Each time think that the encounter has already happened. Pay attention to the enamoured couples everywhere and feel happy for them Watch romantic comedies and movies about love.

Carefully formulate your intention, thank the universe every day for the encounter with your ideal partner. Focus your attention on a specific image of your second half. Feel confident that you will meet him or her in the right time, in the right place. Follow your instincts, listen to your intuition. If you are unexpectedly invited to some event, listen to your inner voice: if it tells you to go, it means that there is some value for you.

Having defined your desires, you will attract their manifestation:

- Thanks for the encounter with my soul mate

- Thanks for the happy family

If you want someone of your relatives to meet his or her second half or to improve the relations in the family, you can also influence the situation by sending love or even by visualizing happiness for the newfound couple.

I have witnessed an interesting course of events. One of my friends has shared her worries about a relationship with a man, or more precisely, about the uncertainty of their future. Ambitious, young and beautiful couple, having achieved a lot in the career, and most importantly, being in love with each other, they could not find a compromise in the question of family. She lived and worked in Finland, he - in Estonia. Both had great opportunities in their countries, and none of them was willing to relocate. My friend has accepted and understood the situation itself. Positive thinking, the faith that everything would get better led her to the encounter with a Neuro-linguistic programming (NLP) specialist in a train compartment. They started talking about the principles of the universe and psychology in general. An expert advised her to write down the desires, on the basis of which a plan of materialization would be made. And less than in a year, my friend and her beloved one have formed a happy family in Finland. The head of the family has been offered a good job, and the happy wife became pregnant.

Let me tell you an interesting story from the life of our handsome Scottish Fold cat. Men, by the way, make a note. We were carefully preparing for the next vacations and have found a wonderful home for our kitty for the period of our absence. All together we went to get acquainted with the hospitable hostess. At the threshold we were greeted by another kitty of incredible beauty, which has demonstrated us a sharp look and a proud temper. Our Gavryusha was full of curiosity and immediately moved closer to talk and to become friends. But this was not appreciated. The Lady Kitty, snorting, covering trails, went to be indignant under the sofa. But Gavryusha was not giving up: first he tried to creep from one side and then from another to have a talk, but Lady was adamant and continued to behave aggressively. I want to note, that this young couple did not even think about any pranks. When we got back from the vacation, that pussycat, the heartbreaker had already returned home. We all could only sigh, so much we wished to find such beautiful bride for our cat. As time passed, we began to look for a decent wife for our Gavryusha. We looked over all the options, but did not succeed to find that one unique cat. Finally, I got an email from one nice Russian girl who was looking for a boyfriend for her own girl cat. But when we have made an appointment, it turned out that it was that kitty, Capitolina, which we and our Gavryusha had fallen in love with. What a mystery, isn't it? I don't know, whether we or our cat have attracted her, but here is one of the proofs that the law of attraction works. Scientists have found out, by the way, that brainwaves of cats are always in Alpha mode, which could mean that they are the strongest practitioners in the materialization of the desires? Sometimes for them it's enough just to look at the tasty piece to attract it;).

Get rid of the idea that all men are the same or everyone cheats. The attention you give to these statements strengthens their negative manifestation. Love your close ones for who they are. Take care of them, if you want them to take care of you. Trust if you want to be trusted. Believe that exactly your husband is perfect. Settle knowledge in yourself that your partner is attentive and loving.

But if you are burdened with these relationships, you do not get anything back, have nothing in common, then take a step to the new relationship. The main thing is to tune yourself to the wave of love and it will come to you: either current relationship will move to the new and improved level or you will find a new love. But remember, if a person is present in our life, it has happened for a reason. Take a closer look, first of all, at yourself.

Do not get used to be offended, to quarrel, to accumulate negative and to sort out the relationship, if you want to keep an emotional intimacy. Neither the dishes nor the promises matter! It all depends on our own attitude, whether we value our relationship or not. If the quarrels occur, immediately connect to the channel of love with the words "I love, I love, I love". Within a minute you will want to hug your loved one, and the cause of the quarrel will evaporate, you will no longer remember it, even if you really would want to. There is one nice advertisement of milk production on the Russian television: ""Prostokvashino"- on the table - love in the family!" The most amazing advertising and "Prostokvashino" is the kindest cartoon in the world, in my opinion. Oxymoron comes up in my mind now, where it is possible to absurdly re-play previously spoken or written words. You can place a CD disk with a cartoon or a book "Prostokvashino" on the table, and quarrel will be over.

Family is your kingdom, you are able to influence the atmosphere at home. There is no place for irritability when you are happy and grateful for all you have. A rude or disrespectful behaviour with a child will be never justified, even if he or she has done something wrong. Trust for trust. Love for love. There's no other way. Do not expect that scolding a child will have a positive impact on the development of the situation. The aggression will never be responded by love, much less by an implementation of promises. If you want to have a mutual understanding with the child, then perhaps your attitude needs to be changed. Constructive conversation with your kid, faith that he or she hears you, remembers and makes necessary conclusions - is your tool in raising the child. Do not worry, your child will not become pampered and spoiled because of such attitude, on the contrary, he will become, first of all, the personality, who values love and respect. And you will create a harmonious relationship, full of trust and mutual understanding, which is so important to inoculate since the childhood. If you are an intemperate person, then before scolding a child, repeat mentally the words "I love, I love, I love", - you will feel better, that's for sure! You will find a common language with the child, and he or she will have a happy childhood. Have you ever noticed that the child gets sick after you were refusing to listen to him or yelling at him? Extinguish hurry and impatience in yourself, you should be happy, because you have such wonderful flower of life. Note: when you quietly wait, believe and trust that the child will make his homework, you will get this.

All children are born geniuses. It is important for you to strengthen your bond with the child, as well as to help him or her. Child development experts say that more than 80% of children have the right hemisphere of the brain predominating. This part of the brain is responsible for the subconscious and the unconscious. The left hemisphere is a hemisphere of the consciousness. The leading hemisphere, as a rule, is determined when the child is about three years old. The children who have a right hemisphere more developed are more inclined to a special way of thinking and the creativity. They want to examine everything, to touch and to try. While they are still very young, they like to drop cups, spoons from the table. And this is not because they behave badly, they just like to examine the emotions and reactions of parents. Children, who have more developed left hemisphere, are tending to consider various factors before making a choice. Nevertheless, both of these types need to make great efforts in the areas that are not close to their development, if they do not get some additional training, which would activate the other hemisphere. If the right hemisphere dominates, the child can have some difficulties in the performing of the tasks. If the left side dominates, then drawing or writing can be challengeable. It is vitally important to develop both hemispheres of the brain. Creative or logical tasks performed together with the child will help in this. If the right hemisphere dominates, not what the others say is more important to the child but how they say this, because he or she perceives the world through emotions. Therefore, your irritability will not be substantiated in this case. Children develop a sense of responsibility only by the age of ten. Understanding the nature of brain activity of your child, you will easily recognize a particular behaviour. Let your child enjoy the childhood, time goes so quickly. The children are our teachers.

You want to give birth, and you were made to think that you cannot have children? You find it hard to believe that you will be able to outwit the words of doctors? Rewrite your past on the sheet of paper, filling it with love. Write that ten years ago you were predicted to have a baby on 7th of July of this year or next. Write that in the conclusion of the doctors you are completely healthy and you will have two healthy boys. Even if doctors make a helpless gesture and say that you cannot have children, and the miracle does not occur, do not doubt, that you will become the happy parents. Believe yourself, your forces, believe that you can influence your destiny. Visualize, how you together with the relatives are watching a video of your family holiday, visualize joint walks and games with the child. Send love to the situation itself, to the causes of the situation, even if you do not know what led you to this problem. Ask saints for help, find an icon and ask them to grant you a baby. My tummy happily rounded because every time my dear mother approached the icon, hanging above our door, appealed to it with the words: "God, make so that my daughter would give up her extreme hobbies and give her a child". Travel into the places of power, which help to prepare the body, to align the emotional level and to get pregnant. Visualize every day that your child is looking at you with happy eyes, how he or she is crawling on a carpet, babbles and laughs.

If the appearance of a child is delayed for some reason, do not despair. It happens that the inner fighting is interfering, and you should finish some matter before the long-awaited little-one will appear in your life. If you cannot manage the emotions, cannot understand, what kind of mission you should carry out first, then refer, again, to the saints so that they would prompt and help to understand yourself. The state of mind after visiting a church is as if you would have been born again.   The sincere and emotional purification happens, you get a feeling of safety and limitless love, with a help of which a person becomes tuned to the divine light.

For a harmonious relationship is important to love yourself. Before you will meet with your beloved, be sure to become cleansed and freed from the blocks of offenses and disappointments. Prepare a place in your life for another person, be ready for a change in your heart. Help yourself with the words "I love, I love, I love" , they will facilitate your way.

Any problem, even in the past, can be solved by love. Wake up with a smile, be glad to the new day, and inspire yourself by a state of happiness, creating the necessary vibrations around you for the attraction of your second half and family creation.

WORK

Your dream job, a position, a decent salary are entitled to be present in your life. The main thing is to determine the goal. Whom do you see yourself, what does your job look like, what kind of people is around you, what are you wearing? Pay attention to the fact that accurate look is a guarantee of success. And this not just because the prospective employer will assess your ability to dress and look neat, but also because in the clothes which emphasize your individuality (in a decent way, of course), you will feel yourself more than a simple worker.

Step by step one develops confidence in himself. Each step makes him more confident, more daring, and more experienced. I do not deny that there are people who already at school feel the strength to achieve heights and, having a healthy impudence, soon become successful leaders or businessmen. Knowing the principles of the law of attraction, a settled understanding of career growth can be reduced significantly. Your Curriculum Vitae should be your business card, after reading it the employer should agree to all your terms. It must be your presentation, your advertising, carefully prepared. You can make it yourself or ask someone to help you to choose wisely the right information. Make a brand of your name, emphasize your advantages.

Clearly and consistently composed resume will, first of all, give you a confidence in getting the desired position, and, secondly, will simply magnetize an attention of your future supervisor both to your resume and to yourself. Complement your presentation by any interesting facts. Describing your work experience, add the details about your duties at the previous places of work. You will make a good impression, if you are able to provide references, recommendations, letters and reviews from your former employers or clients. But if you do not have them, use the social networks such as linkedin.com, which connects millions of specialists of different areas from all over the world. Find your former colleagues and ask them politely to give you recommendations.

Your resume must contain a photo of professional quality. Enter the desired position and salary. Give the facts, the arguments, which will prove that you really are a good specialist. You need to prepare this part carefully and with all responsibility. Re-write, think, read, re-write again, supplement until you are completely satisfied with the text. Your resume, its design, the title should be evident. With the help of the well-comprised and thoroughly designed resume you will feel yourself in the thoroughly planned situation and will be able to get even better position than the one you aspired to.

When your resume is ready, contact the employer. Your goal is to get an invitation for the interview. We take responsibility for what is happening and we write an intermediate goal:

- I am invited for the interview

Fill your resume with energy of love. Mentally create the light around it or send love with the words: "I love, I love, I love". Re-read the resume several times, anticipating an employer's consent to meet with you. With the words "I love, I love, I love" send your resume and do not worry about anything.

As I have already mentioned, when we were searching for a job for my husband, we were getting one rejection after another, so I began to use the Silva Method. While being in the state of Alpha, on the count of 7 I mentally opened a door with number 7, and then opened a door with number 6 and so until the first door, after opening which I found myself on a flower meadow, filled with the sunlight, where all our wishes have already come true.

Before the interview study the practice of the Silva Method. Coming to the meadow, where you have a successful career, fill everything around yourself with light and love. Images and words in the relaxed state of mind programme the brain! You can also mentally play the course of the interview. At the end of such session get activated by the reverse counting: from one to seven.

The next interim goal is to pass successfully the interview and to get the vacant position. Not just some work, but the concretely indicated position or activity. The intermediate objectives are:

- I make a good impression on the employer

- I emit light, healthy mind, confidence

- I speak loudly, clearly, my story is interesting

- The employer is listening to me attentively

- My answers are competent and interesting

- I have enough facts and arguments that are interesting to the employer

The main goal:

- I got the position, I have dreamt about!

My day begins from the previous evening, when before the sleep I begin to program my future morning. Even if I have only four hours left to sleep, I intentionally visualize myself as cheerful, well rested and great looking in the morning. If nevertheless an idea of "so little sleep is not enough" overpowers me, I use plan B: "I will become cheerful, happy, well rested and great looking after the morning shower!" Your day can be also pre-filled with the state of success and happiness, the state of being satisfied with yourself as well as with the planned meetings.

On the day of the interview send love to yourself, to the future employer, to the office, and to the people you meet on your way. Smile to everyone, create a favourable atmosphere.

Emit love during the interview itself. Mentally present a yacht to the person, who interviews you or comb his or her hair (mentally, of course), probably she or he has forgotten to do this being nervous before the interview with such an expert like you.

An important point. Keep in mind that you do not have to be tied to the goal. Calm confidence is your reliable partner in any business. You have to be determined, but at the same time confident to the complete inner peace. If your confidence is overblown, you thereby create the excess potential that will provoke the forces of balance, and you will not get the desired results. You should be happy here and now, be grateful for what you have in your everyday life, rather than focus that you will become happy, having done such an enormous work.

My husband was worried after the examination on the Finnish language: it was difficult, questions were tricky, and he did not have time to answer the audio- test. I told him not to worry, but to use the following technique of the "release" of the situation: "If I have not pass the exam, it's okay, but it would be better if I have passed it". He also needed to throw the experiences away from his mind and just believe that everything was going as it should, with the benefit for all. "Replacing worries by the energy of love, it is possible to create the situation, where the verifier will not pay attention to your mistakes", - I concluded as a loving wife. The test results exceeded all our expectations.

Free yourself from the importance of your intentions:

- If I do not obtain this job, it's okay, but it would be better, if I got it

In any case, believe that everything that happens will propel you towards your goal. The easier you treat a dream, the easier it will be to visualize and achieve its manifestation in your reality. All the great things are simple!

Having moved to Helsinki, I could not get used to the way of 20 km to my new work and the traffic jams, where sometimes I had to spend one hour and a half. Our concern had another brand new office towering proudly near the highway. The walls were made of glass, the frames gilded ☺; the sun was sparkling in the washed, even "licked", windows. I drove this road again and again and one day I decided to try to move into this office. There were no traffic jams at that place and it would take me only 10 minutes to drive there from home. In addition, the office was situated next to the work place of my husband. I went to my boss to discuss the moving. He was very surprised, and stated loudly that in that office on the highway worked only the "privileged"! I was not hurt, but hooked up. "Well", - I thought, "I will use the power of thought then!"

Every time passing by that building I imagined how I was among the privileged, knocking with the heels along the corridors there and looking from the modern glass building on the small cars on the highway. I did not think about the position or the salary. I just clearly saw myself in that building. I firmly believed (in spite of the company's policy) that I would work there. Six months later I was looking for the vacancies in our concern out of curiosity, and suddenly came across the position that seemed interesting to me. Having unexpectedly passed the selection, I found myself in that building, and precisely in that wing where half a year ago I "heard" the sound of my heels!

Having worked there for a year I was pleased with my salary, but I have gained enough experience and felt that it was time to move to the next level. At the private meeting with my new (privileged!) supervisors I noted that my level of knowledge and experience allowed changing the "numbers" in my monthly salary. While the authorities were piercingly looking at me, I also continued to look into their eyes, smiling and repeating in my mind: "I love, I love, I love". After the pause I heard: "This spring due to the general instability of the economic situation, it will not come out, but in the fall you can count on the promotion". In autumn I again started to send love. The rise took place without any trouble.

Once, when I had an important project one of the master servers suddenly has fallen out, and the customer was very serious. Moreover, the specialists who supplied the software, knew that the platform was not quite adapted, although the system is critical. "Nothing can be done", I thought, turning to the usual perception of the world. It was Thursday, the end of the workday, things were very bad, so we appointed a conference call in the morning of the next day. In panic I asked our server management team to reboot the server. In a second another specialist called me and shouted that it had been always prohibited to reboot the server and what wood goblin I had given such instructions. The machine would never boot again! I knew that if I did not take this into my hands, I would be in a big trouble. All Thursday evening I mentally cuddled the servers, wrapped them with love. I admit that I did not feel a real love for them, but repeated: "I love, I love, I love". The next morning I continued to work with the energy of love, sending it already to the shouting and not shouting experts, as well as to our customer. Adrenaline nevertheless rolled to the throat just before the meeting. We began the conference, discussed the recent work of the programs, and suddenly, what a miracle, the customer and our specialist unanimously declared: "It is strange, but something happened during the night, the server has never worked so well for the last two years!" I was triumphant. Of course, I mentally thanked all the participants and my servers for such creative collaboration!

Earlier I gave an example of a quantum transition, when having overcome the indignation, I converted it into the creative energy through the power of destructive energy and got the position I dreamt about. I was preparing for a job interview. My resume has been carefully prepared, and all possible questions for the psychological test and the interview were reviewed in the Internet in advance. I was moved by the same powerful force that transforms energy.

Let's speak of the most powerful energies that help us and push us forward. I'm a woman, and therefore I am familiar with this force, it is an instinct for us. Men also use it, but I believe, in their own way. I am talking about the sexuality power. Not about a vulgarity, but namely about the internal creative force! When we consciously use it, we can work wonders, all the doors are open for us: in the business, relationship, work etc. Sexual energy is sublimated in creativity, it can be also used, when there is a need to attract money. When we are sexually active, we generate a lot of life force energy. I think you will agree that with a help of the sexual energy we can transform all negative into positive. You can program getting the job or any other desire. It is possible to intentionally tune to the channel of this energy to promote any business. Here, again, it is essential to love ourselves in order to emit the necessary fluids (it is not a question of trivial flirtation).

I mentioned earlier, that in sociology there are such concepts as the casual-personal, social-consultative and public spaces or environments, the core of which is the person himself. Imagine yourself inside all these circles, more precisely your power, let it be, for example, in the form of light. What you emit will be reflected in your casual-personal space, which includes the people close to you, things that surround you. Everything you emit through your casual-personal environment will be reflected in your social-consultative space. There are your colleagues, neighbours, friends, places you visit, events, and in our case, the situation of getting the desired position. Next your inner light will be reflected in your distant space, where everything happening is not personal, but you know about it. Consciously using our inner power, we directly start the mechanism, which influences the world around us, creating all necessary conditions and events in it. Having the powerful force inside us, we will fill all the levels of our space with the magic light and will create an atmosphere of positive activity.

Interacting in society, we sometimes create not quite favourable environment by our prejudices and fears. It seems that we are sociable, friendly, but only in our casual-personal environment, because there we feel safe. However, when we get into a social-consultative space as, for example, when we participate in the meeting, where the most part of people does not interact directly with us in the daily work, suddenly we begin to feel some discomfort and constraint. But if we understand the psychology of this kind of interaction, we will be able to identify the problem. Going to a meeting, we set as a goal through the intention:

- I am in complete safety

- I feel comfortable with people around me

A wonderful Soviet/Russian animated film "Hedgehog in the Fog" is an excellent example of how an echo of the gained experience, which pops up in our mind, creates the situations frightening us when we find ourselves in the unusual environment. But if you look closely, something that has suddenly scared you, in fact, is not dangerous at all. Having accustomed yourself to relax and trust the flow of life, even when the fog has covered everything and you do not know what to do, you get what you were looking for:

- I am relaxed and trusting the flow of life, let everything become solved by itself

" Let the water carry me..." - thought the Hedgehog when he fell into the river. He was immediately caught by someone and a minute later he was on the shore, where the Bear was anxiously waiting for him.

We are always short of time. Once, one specialist shared his observations with me: "I do not understand the directors who grab a pile of papers, laptop and rush like a mad along the corridors, demonstrating their significance and busy condition". Have you imagined this picture? Does it seem to you that hurry is actually far-fetched? We demonstrate the lack of time and are afraid of overload. In reality, we get used to such kind of protection, letting people know that we are busy, we do not have time. The law of attraction comes into force and begin to attract more work for us. Hurry creates stress, and stress causes diseases. It is important to recognize the problem and to find the solution:

- I have such a volume of work, that I have time to do everything

Say this phrase at work and at home, and you will notice that these wonderful changes will not take long to wait. Of course, your assistant here is a thorough planning of the business days. You can simply make a list of the matters for each day, which you agree to carry out, spending an hour or two on each task. Or you can be creative in the planning of your day or the some process. In the Internet you can download absolutely free an associative map called FreeMind, it is easy to use.

Having put some task in the centre of the map, add the rays to it, the so called components, by breaking the main goal into the intermediates. For example, you need to promote and sell your goods. Give your product some memorable name that only you will know. Put the name in the middle of the associative map. Now specify the intermediate targets:

- to study the market

- to make a business proposal

- to prepare a selling slogan

- to plan the costs

etc.

Continue to make the following levels of the intermediate goals, for example:

- to study the market

  - to gather the information

    - who can be a customer?

      - how a customer makes the purchasing decision?

      - What determines the behaviour of the customers in the market?

      - When and where will your product be bought more likely?

    - How many customers will you have?

  - To study the prices at which other similar products are sold

Having a responsible attitude towards work, you will feel yourself a valuable employee. Your brain, sending this kind of electromagnetic pulses into your environment, will create an atmosphere of acceptance and with it the successful completion of the undertaking.

Having identified the main goal as a "success", you add the branches with the names to it, which are directly associated with success: recognition, stability, good relationship, equality and an acceptable volume of work. Specify also "decent salary", but be sure to indicate the exact amount that you want, for example, 7 000 € per month. Nothing prevents you from pointing 20 000 €, 100 000 € per month or even more. Then draw the next level's branches. For example, to the "decent salary" you can add:

- the abundance

- the motivation

Continue until you are completely satisfied with the list: abundance - > possibilities - > buying a house - > holidays - > friends. You will identify your desires, and this will help to create the necessary intentions:

- We have great friends and we arrange wonderful holidays in our luxury house

- We live in the abundance, and our possibilities are unlimited

- I am successful, and I make 20 000 € a month, my salary is constantly increasing

Again, ask and it will be given. You just have to identify your desires and trust the universe. Yes, the necessary actions will need to be taken, undoubtedly, to achieve the desired results, but, believe me, when you really want something, the universe will guide you to the right chain of events. You will meet the right people and act with great enthusiasm.

The work should bring you pleasure, first of all. "Choose a job you love, and you will never have to work a day in your life", - Confucius said.

Expand your mind and the horizons of your possibilities by the powers you were given from your birth. Your abilities are a generous gift.

OWN BUSINESS

Constantly working with the subconsciousness and developing thus the cooperation with yourself, you will achieve the level, when the main and intermediate goals, will suddenly start to float up in your mind by their own. You will train the imagination, understanding your limitless possibilities and the vision of the materialized desires. You will find yourself and you will feel confident in the choice of your business.

Where is a calling, is a recognition, and where is a recognition, is your calling. Look for your calling, be happy and successful! Glance at your childhood, what did you love to do? Visit your future, where all your desires have already materialized. You travel a lot, you have absolutely everything: the house, the yacht and the plane. What are you doing in your future?

Our possibilities are limitless, hence we can do whatever we want and we can have whatever we want. "The great breakthrough in your life", - says the legendary Brian Tracy, "comes when you realize that you can learn anything to accomplish any goal that you set for yourself".

Just a couple of years ago it was quite strange and interesting for me, how a young businessman seriously and successfully deals with the activity of several companies, which operate in absolutely different areas. Now I understand that the passion inspired the entrepreneur, and literally opened all the doors in front of him. It excited his mind, causing interest in many different fields of activity. And you also should not limit yourself to one direction: you can be a pilot, a French teacher, an actor, a writer, a toastmaster or a blogger! Go ahead and learn the necessary information, sign up for the courses of landscape design, enter the university to become a doctor. It is never too late to start doing something that really attracts you.

As you remember, the universe takes care of the financial side, if a person does what he or she likes. I will tell you why. When you create with the love, the power of this energy is emitted by you, by your business, transforming your environment into the creative energy. Interacting with the world through the creativity and love, you get into harmony with the Source. You open the parallel reality, the quantum particles, where all the components, including yourself, some objects, your family, clients, traffic, weather and so on, begin to function fully. The harmony reigning everywhere captures all the areas of your life, including the financial one.

I have already suggested you to start a blog. Let us discover its technical side, the promotion and management strategy. In order "to find feet", I advise you to begin from the free resources such as "Blogger" or "Wordpress". I started from "Blogger", but later moved to "Wordpress", which helped me afterwards to build my blog on a paid resource, based on it. I remember my first attempts in writing the posts. I was, apparently, not committed enough to do this seriously. When the specific goal and the confidence, that all necessary information will come itself, have appeared in my life, I desperately began to study the principles of the blog. Put forth that the information would come free, and it will happen. But of course both free and paid seminars, in any case, will be useful for you. You will be charged with the necessary energy, will get the right motivation and detailed briefing. Understanding the structure of these activities, it will be easier to cover the entire ensemble of the work of blogger, understand the necessary action plan and run the blog itself.

The real earnings are possible when there is a full-fledged website. You can also make money on the page of your group in the social networks. The advertisers will get interested in the popularity of your group and will contact you with a request to place a sponsored link on your page. However, promotion of your group and attraction of thousands of subscribers will also require some investments from you. Contact the administrators of the popular groups to arrange your reference in their news section. Certainly, the content of your own group must already be at the high level and should be interesting to the new subscribers.

Having decided to start a blog, take the full responsibility: well-run blogs and groups in the social networks have about fifty posts a day.

You can also schedule blog posts to be published automatically at any time. The regular posting of articles will be beneficial for the rapid indexing of your site by the search engines.

In order not to tire the reader, use maximum 100 characters in each post. Always quote a source when you publish other people's articles or photos. Respect your reader, do not abuse blog by only advertising, publish efficient and interesting information.

Create the vivid images/motivators, which will make others want to like them and to publish on their own walls. Publish polls and competitions among your readers. Make friends with the sister groups.

Make a list of the required regular activities for each day, for example: a status update, writing articles, adding the images/motivators, inviting new people, publishing your own links on the similar sites, adding photos, making a poll or competition, asking the readers some provocative questions and so on. Having a goal and performing the necessary actions every day, you will achieve the popularity of your websites.

Let's return to the writing of a post in your blog. Here are few tips, carrying out which, you will gain an optimization of the texts for the search engines:

- The key phrase is required to be contained in the title of the post

- The key phrase should appear multiple times within your text

As for the external optimization, the purpose of which is the withdrawal of the pages to the maximum possible positions in the search engines and the attraction of readers and subscribers, here you need to increase the reference mass. Select two or three resources of adjacent thematic, become a user and start to comment actively, giving a link to your site, signing by the keyword of your blog.

You can have your blog or a channel on youtube. You can conduct your seminars or write a book, the choice is yours! Do not be afraid to try yourself in different areas. If you have not written anything before, it does not mean that you will not be able to release your first book to the world. Information will come to you as soon as you feel the excitement. It is worth to start doing something in your life for the dream, and everything around will begin to promote your occupation, inspiring you more and more to the work and creativity.

Let my book be a clear example and an incentive for writing your own work. Create your humorous guidebook about Russia or any other country, where you have been. Write about "the secrets of happy blonde" or "healthy nourishment step by step". There are many ideas, pick the one that will be personally yours, which will "purr" for you. Remember that your goal will remain alive, if you spend an hour or two on it each day, until your business becomes your basic activity. The thought generates the action, and the action creates the result!

MONEY

Oddly enough, but in the section of money I'd like to talk about the spirituality and the nobility of our soul. In the essence, following the simple rules of life, when all the negative emotions step back, we are cheerful, friendly and merciful, we enrich the spiritually. We become more loving, not only to others, but also to ourselves. Being able to see the beauty here and now, to appreciate it, we begin to interact harmoniously with all the energies in the universe, and all spheres of life reach a new level. The power of money also belongs to the power of creation. Our spiritual and material growths are inseparably connected with each other. Money is just a component of our life, it is energy, with a help of which we obtain the manifestation of the desired things. When our mind is not blocked by the prejudices about the money, we allow this energy to flow into our life. We enjoy life, we are kind to people, we prosper and with us our environment begins to flourish too. Would you agree that it is better to be rich and healthy, than poor and sick?

Visualizing yourself with such amount of money that you can afford everything you want, you are creating the new circumstances in your life. It doesn't matter for the universe if you are imagining something real or not, it takes your images as though they already exist.

Become a magnet for the money, believe in this with every cell of your body. The constraint to think freely about money will not lead you to the desired result, so develop a sense of lightness and joy, when you think about it. Learn to control your thoughts, and you will get close to the success. Emotions and thoughts are inseparable. Attention has a memory and returns back to us, so when you once again pay your bills in the bank, make sure you are glad that you have money for this, that you can give away the necessary amount with ease. Remember that the happy thoughts are stronger and more effective than negative. By your positive attention to the money, you can attract wealth into your life.

"Imagine yourself as a magnet for money", probably, you have heard this phrase many times. I would like to add only one word here, which will remove all the blocks and will take you to the way of the money attraction into your life. Imagine yourself as a magnet for **the energy** of money! Think about the colour of this energy, which will be easy to perceive and receive. I see this energy with a golden hue, with a soft and warm light. Wrap yourself by this energy, imagine how it comes into your life, filling everything around. Sense it inside yourself so that you feel comfortable and pleasant. Connect to it using your energy of love, feel how you merge into one.

I have been asked many times, how to imagine this energy, where it comes from, and how to visualize it "correctly ". Do not create any complications and limitations. It all depends on you, it will appear in the manner you think it should appear! Let it be a column of light from space, from the hands of an angel or from a jug. You do not need visualize the source, it's enough to imagine the energy.

Constantly repeat to yourself, that you are rich, with a feeling of gratitude and joy. It will take very little time, and you will see the manifestation of energy of money in your life. Do not waste a minute on your worries, go to the new and improved level right now.

Never reject help, even if you are offered ten euros. Do not block the channel of energy of money. Accept help with gratitude. Help those who need it, but when you give money, do it with a joy, - you will definitely get all back.

If you have lost money, know, this is a sign that they will come to you from some other source. Breath in the energy of money, let it flow freely in your life. Change not only your thinking, but also your behaviour, even your gait. Train a confidence that you will live in abundance.

Always wish a specific amount of money. I was repeating "thanks for 2 000 €", and one day our neighbour came to us with the news that everyone in our housing cooperative will get back 2000 €. A miracle, by attracting a necessary amount of money to my family, I have made a gift of the same sum to all the neighbours. My environment was enriched too.

Be fearless in your desires. Ask the universe for millions. Ask to give a requested amount to everyone in your environment, not forgetting about magic words "with the benefit for all", and you will attract the right circumstances, which will create the conditions for your enrichment and for the welfare of your close ones. Wish new acquisitions and money not only for yourself, but also for your environment.

I often hear: "Someone can attract money by the power of thought, but others cannot". In the essence, absolutely everyone can develop the ability not to live by poor expectations. For example, you are practicing already the power of thought, you are tuned on the money energy flow, but you receive a bill with a large sum of money, and you again are in despair. I note that you can congratulate yourself with the best practice of the power of thought, when the low spirit doesn't bother you anymore, and you easily pay the bills, knowing that you can afford to pay it. Then the same amount of money will come to you from "nowhere". The dismay reinforces the lack of money, and joy is the attention, which energy of money loves. Therefore it will be more reasonable to be glad for the bills, since they are the signs that you are able to pay them. And, according to your belief, new earnings will not be long in coming.

I live in a country where the tax percentage increases according to the income. Such policy can stop someone in the desire to reach a higher financial level but, identifying a target, we can reach it easily:

- My income is so large that I do not care what tax I have to pay to the government

Vadim Zeland reveals the theme of "swaying of the pendulum": negative thinking reinforces the manifestation of something we do not want, and positive, correspondingly, attracts happy changes into our life by the certain thoughts, which swing the nature of the situation to one side or another. If we do not madly celebrate our victory, then disappointment from the defeat will not occur. The forces of balance will be maintained, and the preservation of the vacuum of gratitude and love around our desire will create the reliable conditions for its manifestation. If we are unhappy because of the coming bills, we attract the additional sources, and being distressed, we swing the pendulum of lack of money. Take each new bill in your hands and before opening it rejoice to a new source of income. Fill the envelope, your wallet and the bank account with love. Opening the envelope, visualize, that you got a notice about a refund. Get used to open each new envelope with the thoughts: "Great, the money has come!" Even if there is a bill, you will get a feeling that a required amount of money is coming to you to pay it. Positive attention to the money, steady and favourable swaying of the pendulum will lead to the fact that you "get stuck" in good. When we returned from a two week holiday, there was a surprise at home: four hundred envelopes with the bills were waiting for us! My reaction to the appearance of the bills had been already trained: "Wow, what a wealth!" - I exclaimed. As it turned out, all the bills were sent to us by mistake. I could seek a compensation for such a surprise, but I simply decided that it was enough to get a sufficient sign: we were such a prosperous family that we were able to pay even all those bills.

Now, when you consciously started to apply the principles of the law of attraction, you will observe and notice the changes as well, even your small victories. Having experienced the impact of the power of thought, you will pay more attention to your thoughts and beliefs, and with them, to your dreams and intentions, and this undoubtedly, will lead you to the achievement of the goal.

Use the following intentions:

- I am happy about any positive manifestations in my life

- I have everything I want, and I am grateful for it

- I interact harmoniously with the energy of money

Write a letter full of admissions, addressed to the energy of money. Having sincerely laid out your emotions on paper, you will get free from the interfering beliefs. And by paying attention to the money through this letter, you will open the channel of its receiving. Here is an example of such rotation with the use of Ho'oponopono technique:

"How do you do, my dear energy of money, I am so glad, that I can now write to you. **I'm sorry**, I had not talked to you earlier, and I didn't let you enter my life because of my own prejudices. Now everything will be different, my doors and windows are opened for you. You are always welcome. **Please, forgive me** that I did not try to meet you before, and I did not believe that I can so openly admit my feelings for you. I did not know how to receive and spend you correctly, because it was always not enough of you, I was offended with you and did not understand what I was doing wrong. **Thank you** that you did not nevertheless leave me, but has manifested in my life, when I needed you. I am grateful for your love to me and my wealth. Now, having realized that our relationship depended on my world view, I will pay more attention to you through my sincere gratitude for any your manifestations. I call you into my life by my open mind, my heart, because **I love you**, and we cannot be split."

Lottery is a good option. There is a saying: if you want a lot of money, to begin with, play a lottery. In the book "The Messenger" Klaus Joehle describes a technique by which he partially earns his living - the lottery winnings. You should relax, turn on the sounds of train and visualize yourself on some station where you buy a tomorrow's newspaper. Then you return to the train, while you are going home in your visualization, you memorize the numbers of tomorrow's lottery. This is a simple method, but you need to be a skilful creator to have this kind of the habit of visualization. In any case I'm not trying to dissuade you. If you set a goal, you will certainly achieve it. But if you see the lottery as the only way to become rich, you thereby create the restrictions, unconsciously blocking the channels of other possible and impossible sources of income. Even playing a lottery, do not specify more than one row of numbers, it will be enough. If visualisation was correct, you will win with only one row of numbers, right? But do not make the victory in a lottery an objective in itself or the only way of enrichment. Try it as a game, filling the entire process from the entering of numbers to the lottery with energy of love. You can also notice the harmonious interaction with the energy of money when, for example, leaving for the vacation with your family to the sea, you fill the lottery ticket, and on the arrival home you suddenly discover a lottery win. You have happily spent time together with the family, enjoyed socializing and lightness in relationship, you became cheerful and well rested. Do you see the key of your well-being? You are here and now experiencing the feeling of happiness, you are grateful for the sky, the sun, the family and the friends, and you enter the harmony with the world around you, where your desires begin to come true. And I do not mean that it is necessary to go to the sea for happiness, but I bring you an example of a favourable interaction between a human and the universe and its gifts.

Trips bring useful impressions, they are the investments, which in reality justify themselves. Do not regret that you have spent money without any profit. After all, you wanted to travel, and hence, the money for the journey came to you for a reason. Before the trip I always ask the universe to provide me bank savings, so that when I return, I do not have to worry about the financial side, while I enjoy the memories of the wonderful places. We get what we ask for.

All the investments and acquisitions should evoke positive emotions, which can and should be created in ourselves consciously. A professional salesman, for example, will contact a buyer of an expensive car after the deal and, by correctly comprised questions that cause positive emotions, will make sure that the client is happy with his new acquisition, praising, of course, the advantages of the car, and, giving thus the client a confidence in the correctness of his choice.

Money love calculation. Spend them respectfully: by necessity or when you feel that the thing, you liked so much, is "yours". Rejoice when spending money. Feel the significance of your investments. Save money to buy something in order to avoid the consumption of the energy of debts.

Motivate yourself to wealth! Always have a large banknote with you, but do not spend it. Keep an eye in a store on everything that you could buy on that amount. Help the wealth to find a way to you– there will be more money, and you will become happier. Feel free to let yourself have a decent stable income with a clearly indicated amount:

- My income is 20 000 euros per month

Read more about business and marketing and attend the seminars of successful people. Meet the enterprising, cheerful people. Discuss the ideas, ask for advises. Turn your knowledge and skills into the money. Ask a reliable person to become your companion, at least for the first couple of years. It is fun to start business together, and you will more responsibly regard the common work.

Every day spend time on developing your consciousness of money, making and complementing the lists of your desires, without limiting yourself in any way. Dream, visualize yourself as the owner of an island or a luxury yacht. Think of joint evenings with your favourite actors, who live next door. By making the lists on a paper, you will develop in yourself not only the skill to reveal and to compose the desires, but to visualize them, you will gain confidence in their materialization. Indeed these thoughts, feelings and emotions are necessary to achieve the goals. Remove limitations, but remain humane, it is possible to succeed without losses, when there is a balance of material and spiritual.

His Holiness Dalai Lama has left the sea of light, inner peace and happiness after his visit to Helsinki. I listened to his every word, and every word was perceived by energy, emotions and love. I was dissolved in his positive, magic energy and good feelings penetrated more and more to everything that surrounded me in life. His Holiness touched upon the topic of money: "Money is good, further development is not possible without money". At the same time he noted that it is a mistake to think that money is all, a man, first of all, must find peace of mind and harmony. Only in this case he will attract welfare. The main thing is a healthy, positive mind.

JOURNEYS

Do you want to travel a lot? Then you only need to tell the universe about that. Yes, so simple. This is the way to get money for your journeys. Decide first where you want to go: what place you are planning to visit and when. Speaking of the dates. Re-reading "I'm Magnet", I came across the horoscope for my mother. It is clear that no one has read my book yet and nobody knows that I have made a horoscope. There was a trip predicted for her in March, and actually, exactly in March she visited Prague. So, we can conclude that the horoscope is accurate, and the planned event, as a rule, is achieved to the date indicated.

Water has a memory, and it is not surprising that during morning jogging or walking along the coast, the water attracts and turns our mind to interact with it. In my meditations I often go mentally to the sea to rest and gather strength. The sea does not let me go, it is calling for me, when we are waiting for the next holiday. Therefore, I love to travel and I like to discover new places and new coasts.

I really wanted to see fabulous Nice, to feel it as it is on pictures. But I was delirious about the trip to completely different place. A picture, where I am racing in a cabriolet along the sea, and a kerchief on my head is fluttering merrily, began to appear in my mind by itself. It excited my brain by its unobtrusiveness, ease and beauty. I liked to return to it in my thoughts, something fairy-tale and unconstrained was in it. The picture helped me even to transform my mood into a state of some zero gravity, - the mind connected to the game in the association. And although it appeared more and more often, I was not still connecting its appearance with the real journey to Nice. A trip to the country, to which I longed to go, did not want to "be organized", something always interfered. And then during one of our friendly gatherings a neighbour suddenly declared, that he was sent to me (by someone from above) to transmit important message: "Do not rush things, everything has its time". And then even more interesting: "Go to Nice". Of course, no one knew about my picture of a cabriolet and fluttering kerchief. His words have helped me to put everything together. I caught some important meaning of these parting words and boldly booked a trip to Nice. Oh, what a happy moment it was when I suddenly found myself in the picture, which was once simply a thought!

In Nice and its environs I have discovered the amazing places that made my heart beat faster. I fell in love with French soulfulness and beauty, and... was inspired to write a book.

If you want to see the Eiffel Tower, get pictures, look them through every day, imagine what you will see strolling around Paris. Listen to the songs about Paris, say out loud:

" Bonjour, Madam/ Monsieur, pardon,

excusez-moi, salut, merci,

s'il vous plaît,

Paris,

Je t'aime,

C'est belle journée,

C'est la vie!"

(An improvised verse.)

The price doesn't really matter, what is important is a goal you set for yourself. If you want to have a vacation in the Maldives every year, then it can be realized too! Find the pictures of the beaches and hotels, put into this book and view them as often as possible. Think of how you are serenely sipping an exotic cocktail, luxuriate at the shore, how you are strolling on the soft white sand, and the water is caressing your feet.   Mentally meet the rises and the sunsets, admire the beauty and breathe deeply.

Wish Wheel or parting words

When a person suddenly realizes that through the power of thought he can affect the course of events in his life, he certainly wants to affect immediately all aspects of it: to get a dream house, a yacht, to travel a lot, to be always healthy, to have a happy family, to be rich and successful. The concentration of positive thoughts on all the areas at the same time scatters the attention and it does not let to focus on one or two desires.

I want to share my invention with you, it will help you to feel visually and internally the work of the law of attraction and will also become your reliable tool in the materialization of all your plans. You are, of course, familiar with the map of desires or vision board, which, undoubtedly, has a property of attraction. I would like to suggest the use of more powerful tool, which will remind you of the constituent elements necessary for the successful materialization, instil faith and involve you in the joint creative work. The Wheel of the Wishes will open a way to the creative concentration and will create all the conditions for a significant leap forward.

Draw a large circle, divide it into seven identical segments and paint each section. Designate each part by an arrow, symbolizing rotation, and place Wish Wheel in a visible place. Sign each section:

> ➤ Love and family

> ➤ Work

> ➤ Own business

> ➤ Health

> ➤ Journeys

> ➤ Money

> ➤ Relationship

Of course, you might as well choose your own directions and spheres of life.

Put your photo in the centre of this magic tool or materializer. Find some images of your desires in the Internet or cut them out from the magazines and put into the relevant sections of the circle. A house, a yacht or a summer cottage can take place in the section of money, give it direction. You can attach the word "ideas" to "own business" section. Use pictures associated with health on its own section.

Select two most important at the moment sections and concentrate all your attention and energy on the manifestation of these images in your reality. Let them be, for example, the pictures, personifying a happy family and wealth.

Now fill all the pictures with words and energies of love and gratitude. So you will start the mechanism of the wheel rotation, you will enter the gold road of your well-being and prosperity. You will become a rider of the chariot, a master and creator of your life. Having started the movement and given a sufficient attention to the most relevant moments, subsequently, you will be able to decide which area of life needs more frequent visualization without worrying that some of the parts will be unaffected by your thoughts for a while. The engine will become eternal, the rotation will only increase the effects of the forces of love and gratitude, filling them with energy of all your desires, no matter on which part you are currently working. The magnetism of two chosen desires will affect the materialization of all other desires. It is important to support the process of the way, the work of the wheel, regularly sending love and gratitude to your desires.

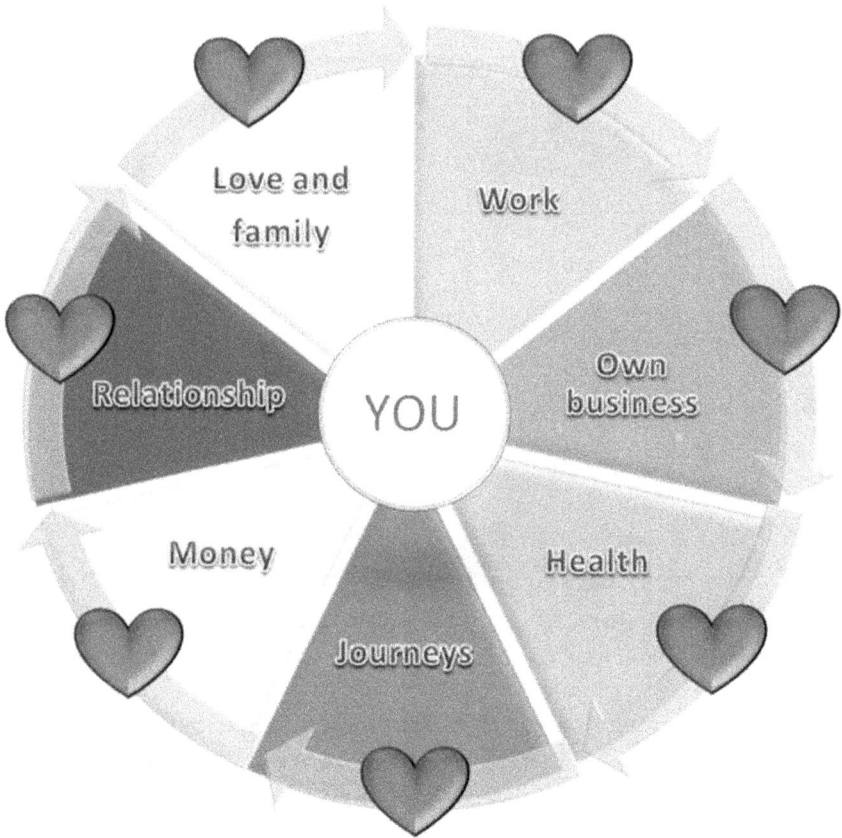

Wish Wheel

Thank you!

I am a happy person, because I am grateful for the life I have and to people close to me, to everyone who exists in my world, whom I have met on my way.

I am grateful to myself for having consciously taken the responsibility for everything that happens in my world, for every day when I find time for my dream. I am grateful for the gift to love.

I say "I love you and thank you" to all my close people and friends. I love and thank my daughter-magician for her laugh, her spontaneity and aspirations. I love and thank my ideal and loving husband for the ability to listen to me and to support, for believing in me. I love and thank my parents for my happy life, for their participation and love. I love and thank my precious mother for the invaluable assistance in the development of our child, for the women's strength, tenderness, intelligence, for all the beauty that she always brings by her appearance. I say: "Thank you my dear for inspiring me to the new achievements, thank you for loving me and my family, thank you for your requests for a happy life for me and your participation in the creation of well-being of our family".

I am grateful to His Holiness Dalai Lama, from whom I have learnt a lot about the penetration, the creativity to the world and all the living things, for the spiritual enrichment. I am grateful to Rhonda Byrne for the awareness of my inner strength. I am grateful to Joe Vitale for his energy and wisdom, for the inspiration that he emits and with which he charges the people. I am grateful To Stive G. Jones for his sincere trainings on NLP. I am grateful to Paolo Coelho for those changes in my life that happened because of his books. I am grateful to Klaus Joehle for understanding of the power of love and to Burt Goldman for a quantum transition.

I am very grateful to my friends Ludmila Sorvoya from Oulu and Marina Morozova from Moscow, who have kindly agreed and provided invaluable assistance in the editing of this book in Russian.

I am very grateful to Julia Zatulo from Sankt-Peterburg who has helped significantly having edited my English version of "I'm Magnet".

I am very grateful to you, my dear readers, that you have made possible the manifestation of this book.

Write me, I will be very happy to receive your feedbacks and mails about your undertakings and successes of any value: book@immag.net.

I wish you the ease and inspirations, let the whole process from the awareness of your desire to its materialization be satiated with positive emotions, joy and love.

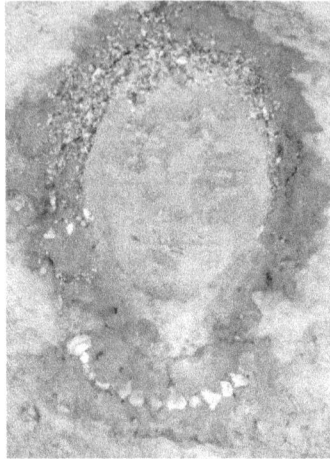

She is looking at the sea with a serene smile of love,

By miracle having arisen from a rock of clay...

She appears from the depths of the soul

When you have achieved the inspirations fires.

- Elena Gushchina

(made on a coastal clay rock on Greek island Kefalonia, 2012)

Epilogue

I have never written a book, but having found a happy inner harmony I got the inspiration that contributed to the realization of the direction in the implementation of creative energy. The book is written intuitively, and therefore, please do not judge it too strictly.

A feeling of happiness inspires. Every day spending just a few minutes to pay attention to all these wonderful moments that happen around us, we can completely change our life.

I'm looking forward to your comments, your amazing stories. Frankly, my biggest dream is to encourage each of you to take an action, to create something you will love or write your own book. Mail me to book@immag.net or leave your feedbacks on the website immag.net.

I am waiting for you!

To be continued...

Diary of gratitude and success

I congratulate you on the successful comprehension of your life!

My goal was not to teach you something new or to change your foundations. Those who practice the power of thought, understand: "I'm Magnet" is a kind of alarm clock, prompting a need for an action and awakening you to use the inner strength through an emotional awareness of your own images, which have arisen during the reading.

You decide where to direct your creative energy. Let this book become your personal assistant. Strengthen its power, which works precisely for you by the gratitude you will add, re-reading, paying attention and at the same time strengthening the energy of the book.

Update your notes in it. Come back each time to the gratitude written previously, re-read and write down your new successes.

I would suggest to you to keep a diary of your further independent work. There you will be able to put a gratitude to the various events and situations in your life, and at the same time to replenish something that brings joy to you. Perhaps in the beginning will not be easy, but let it be at first your little observations that have given you some pleasant emotions: "Grate weather all day" or "Had nice chat with a friend". Subsequently, believe me, feeling good, and learning to notice the good, it will become difficult to stop writing, - remarking everything that the universe sends to you. It is very exciting!

Paying attention to just a few enjoyable moments during the day, you are saying to the universe: "I am grateful for all this!", and it happily multiplies your well-being in response, sending to you even bigger surprises.

Diary of gratitude and success

Diary of gratitude and success

Health

Diary of gratitude and success

Diary of gratitude and success

Relationship

Diary of gratitude and success

Diary of gratitude and success

Love and Family

Diary of gratitude and success

Diary of gratitude and success

Money

Diary of gratitude and success

Diary of gratitude and success

Work

Diary of gratitude and success

Diary of gratitude and success

Own business

Diary of gratitude and success

Diary of gratitude and success

Journeys

Diary of gratitude and success

Books I recommend

- " Essential Reiki" by Diane Stein
- "Illusions" by Richard Bach
- "Life on The Other Side" by Sylvia Browne
- "Love your disease" by Valery Sinelnikov
- "Philosophical Tales" by Kozlov N.I.
- "Sam sebe volshebnik" (rus) by V. Gurangov and V. Dolokhov
- " The Alchemist" and "Brida" by Paulo Coelho
- "The Complete Reiki Course" by Master Naharo, Gail Radford
- "The Hidden Messages in Water" by Masaru Emoto
- "The Messenger" by Klaus J.Joehle
- "The Millionaire's Secrets" by Mark Fisher
- "The Monk Who Sold His Ferrari" by Robin Sharma
- "The Secret" & "The Power" by Rhonda Byrne
- "The Silva Mind Control Method for Getting Help from Your Other Side"by Jose Silva and Robert B. Stone
- "The Silva Mind Control Method Of Mental Dynamics" by Jose Silva and Burt Goldman
- "The Power of Intention" by Valeri Sinelnikov
- "Think and Grow Rich" by Napoleon Hill
- "Reality transferring" by Vadim Zeland
- "Who Moved My Cheese?" by Spencer Johnson
- "Zero Limits" by Joe Vitale, Ihaleakala Hew Len

My Friends

AL PHOTOGRAPHY

www.activelines.net

ANNA GAV JEWELRY

annagav.com

SurvivalTech Nord

www.survivaltechnology.net

GENRE WORKS

www.genreworks.com

Beauty Room BELLAGIO

www.beautyroombellagio.fi

findows

www.findows.fi
www.findows.ru

InnoTrain

www.innotrain.fi

Ludmila Sorvoja

Translation services RUS-FIN

vk.com/id5119981

Julia Zatulo

Translation services RUS-ENG

vk.com/id278006

Tmi Kaisa Sainkangas

www.kaisasainkangas.com

Lydmila Nyman

Life Coaching

goo.gl/nyK9KS

Царские Цацки

vk.com/club53965941

Viarenich Olga photography

goo.gl/8ocMXF

Glam Lady

www.facebook.com/ljubasha.shtepa

Pavel Abramov

Electronic repair services

goo.gl/xRLN05

Nataliya Ukkonen

Dental Technician

goo.gl/XX2O62

To experience more...

immag.net

Elena Gushchina

I'M MAGNET

immag.net
#immagnet
book@immag.net

Book and cover design by Elena Gushchina.

ISBN 978-952-68354-0-2 (Paperback)
ISBN 978-952-68354-1-9 (EPUB)